E. (Edward) Marston

Frank's Ranche

Or, My holiday in the Rockies

E. (Edward) Marston

Frank's Ranche
Or, My holiday in the Rockies

ISBN/EAN: 9783337063375

Printed in Europe, USA, Canada, Australia, Japan

Cover: Foto ©ninafisch / pixelio.de

More available books at **www.hansebooks.com**

FRANK'S RANCHE

OR

MY HOLIDAY IN THE ROCKIES

BEING A CONTRIBUTION TO THE INQUIRY INTO
WHAT WE ARE TO DO WITH
OUR BOYS

BY THE AUTHOR OF
"*AN AMATEUR ANGLER'S DAYS IN DOVEDALE*"

"To thy bent mind some relaxation give.
And steal one day out of thy life, to live!"
COWLEY

Second Edition.

LONDON
SAMPSON LOW, MARSTON, SEARLE, & RIVINGTON
CROWN BUILDINGS, 188, FLEET STREET
1886

(*All rights reserved*)

Oh! happy farmers! overblest I wis,
If they could only realise their bliss!
For whom the earth, away from jingling strife,
In just abundance sheds the gifts of life."
      VIRGIL's *Georgics.*
     (*R. D. Blackmore's Translation.*

DEDICATORY LETTER.

MY DEAR FRIEND M.,

I CANNOT but dedicate this little volume to you who have been my pleasant travelling companion for many thousands of miles in the great western world. But for you I should probably never have undertaken such a journey; and for how many acts of thoughtful kindness by the way am I not indebted to you? Can I forget that you always insisted on my taking the best bunk in the cabin, the best seat in stage-coaches, the best room in hotels, the best bed in sleeping cars? Can I forget that it was your warmhearted friendship for Frank which induced you to "rough it" with me in his little log shanty? And ought I not gratefully to remember the inexhaustible resources of that wonderful travelling bag and the cruse of cordials which, in time of need, were ever at my service? No man could have had a more pleasant, unselfish, and kind companion than you were, and my only regret is that I have not been able to produce a record of our journeyings more worthy of your acceptance.

Yours faithfully,
E. M.

London,
 Christmas, 1885.

INTRODUCTORY NOTE.

HAT can justify one in addressing himself to the general public as if it were his private correspondent?" asks Oliver Wendell Holmes. He then answers his own question by stating that "there are at least three sufficient reasons," and proceeding to give them.

I wish I could with satisfaction to myself offer any one of those three reasons for the existence of this little book. But, I cannot venture to say that I have "a story to tell which everybody wants to hear;" neither have I "been shipwrecked, or been in a battle, or witnessed any interesting event that I can tell anything new about." It is needless to add that I have not been hugged by a bear or scalped by an Indian. I do not presume to assert that I can "put in fitting words any common experiences not already well told;" and so I must assign the third reason, which permits me " to tell anything I like, provided I can so tell it as to make it interesting."

I cling to this third reason; it embodies the only plea I can put forth. I have tried to make my story interesting; it would gratify me deeply to believe that I have succeeded.

"What shall we do with our boys?" is a question frequently put to the body politic through the medium of the newspapers in the dull season. My experience has convinced me that the question is a useless one. You may train up and control your boys to a certain age; you may make them a present of as good an education as you can afford; you may lay down plans for their future; you may find niches for each one to fill; you may fondly hope that each one in his turn will quietly drop into his niche; that they will live and work together, and in course of time become a help and comfort to you in your declining years.

But will they do so? I have other sons

besides Frank, and they have found niches for themselves quite other than the ones I had intended for them when years ago I said to myself "What shall I do with my boys?" Now they have sons and daughters of their own, who will no doubt soon become objects of the same inquiry in their turn.

Frank's erratic wanderings from the niche I had designed for him are recorded in these pages. I have written them in the hope that they may be, if not very interesting, at least useful to young fellows who, like him, cannot rest content in the parent nest, however well-feathered or cotton-woolled it may be; but who also, like Frank, seem to be impelled by some subtle influence, or by—

> "Such wind as scatters young men thro' the world
> To seek their fortune further than at home,
> Where small experience grows."

CONTENTS.

PART I.

LETTER I.—My bright anticipations — Melancholy forebodings—Bound for the Rockies—Frank's start for the Far West—Farming in Minnesota—A new scheme—Starting a creamery—Glowing hopes—Failure and disappointment . . *Page* 1

LETTER II.—Frank's dearly-bought experience—A start for the Rockies—Magnificent scenery—Indian scouts and revolvers—Advice to parents—Frank's determination to "rough it" 11

LETTER III.—A hundred and twenty miles' walk — Axe, pick-axe, and shovel—A four-hundred-feet roll down the mountain—Rough living—An Indian scare—Deadly fumes—Working round a smelter—Fishing in Lake "Abundance"—Disturbed by a grizzly 16

LETTER IV.—Starting afresh on a new farm—Wheat forty to seventy-five bushels to the acre—Felling trees and fencing—"Life here is deuced hard"—Somewhat despondent—Forty below zero—Ink and bacon frozen—Anxiety for General Gordon—Working in snow up to the waist . . . 27

LETTER V.—Never had such a hard time—Camping out in the Rockies—Horses decamp—Left in the lurch—A terrible fright—Crossing a torrent—"Old Jim" taking a roll—Pack smashed—"Old Jim" in a snow-drift—Woke up by a grizzly—What the newspapers said of it—Cutting fencing poles in the snow—Christmas Day—Pickles and plum pudding—The consequences—A dance Cowboys and farmers' daughters—"Shall I turn tail?"—A profitable old cow—The nicest little ranche in Montana—Start on a sheep drive 300 miles—"The healthiest place I ever struck" 35

LETTER VI.—My last letter before leaving for the United States by the good ship "Cunardia" 55

PART II.

LETTER VII.—On board the "Cunardia"—Small troubles—The Romance of a rickety old chair—Arrival at New York—First acquaintance with katydids 57

LETTER VIII.—Up the Hudson River—The Catskills—My first chipmunk—"The Rip Van Winkle"—"Sleepy Hollow"—The Mountain-House Hotel—Old Indian squaw-spirit—A snake in the grass—A painting by Holbein . . . 63

LETTER IX.—Arrival at Saratoga—Season over—Hotel crowded with Deputies for nomination of a State Governor—Mugwump—Arrival at Niagara—The Falls at midnight and by moonlight No letter from Frank 73

LETTER X.—Start for Chicago—" The Michigan Central "—Arrival at Chicago—Still no letter from Frank—Start for St. Paul—St. Paul and Minneapolis—Commodore Kitson's stables—Falls of St. Anthony—" The Granary of the World "—Falls of Minnehaha—Telegram to Frank to meet me at Livingston 82

LETTER XI.—The North Pacific Railway—Brainerd—Detroit—Massacre by Sioux—Indian Reservation—Fargo—Wheat-fields of Dakota—Bismarck—" Bad Lands "—The Rockies—Arrival at Livingston—No news of Frank—My great disappointment 93

LETTER XII.—The Yellowstone National Park—" The New Wonderland "—" The Devil's Slide "—The stage driver—Story of a corpse—Driving a circus coach—Circus Bill " appropriates " a coat—Stealing their own blankets—Start for the Park—Mammoth Springs—Forest of dead pines—The Lake of the Woods—Norris Hot Springs and Geysers—" Hell's Half-acre "—A perilous drive—Fire Hole River—Lower Geyser Springs—" Old Faithful "—" The Bee Hive "—The Grand Cañon—Rough roads—Return—" The Golden Gate "—A strange pedestrian—" By Jove ! it's Frank !" 106

LETTER XIII.—Livingston to Bozeman—Bozeman City—Arrival at Frank's ranche—Frank's progress—The shanty—Kitten and mice—Aroused by a ground squirrel—Variation of climate—A snowstorm—Our beds drenched—" Baching " it—

Shaving under difficulties—Situation—Fertility of the soil—Cultivation of strawberries—Fine grazing district—Climate—Story of our holiday on the ranche—Fishing in West Gallatin river—New bridge and old canoe—"The coloured aristocracy"—Three bear stories 129

LETTER XIV.—Saying " Goodbye "—Departure in a heavy snowstorm — Gallatin Valley — Helena — Garrison—Butte City—Salt Lake City—Polygamy—Articles of faith—Trial of a murderer—Trial of polygamists 160

LETTER XV.— Leave for Cheyenne—"Rock Springs"—Murder of Chinese—Mr. Black's "Green Pastures" and bottle of champagne—"Hell upon Wheels"—Big Horn Cowboy and Milord . 186

LETTER XVI.—We leave Cheyenne—Arrival at Omaha—The barber's shop—Narrow escape from having my head shaved—Arrival at Chicago—Niagara Falls 197

CONCLUSION 202

APPENDIX 205
   How to obtain Government Land . . . 205
   Pre-Emptions 206
   Homesteads 207
   Timber Culture Claims 209
   Desert Land 211
   Government Land Offices 213
   Diagram of Time across the American Continent 214

THE UNITED STATES
OF NORTH AMERICA
Author's Route

FRANK'S RANCHE;

OR,

MY HOLIDAY IN THE ROCKIES.

LETTER No. I.

My bright anticipations—Melancholy forebodings—Bound for the Rockies—Frank's start for the Far West—Farming in Minnesota—A new scheme—Starting a creamery—Glowing hopes—Failure and disappointment.

London, July, 1885.

LAST year I spent a pleasant time in Dovedale, and "The Amateur Angler" told you all about it. This autumn I had looked forward to a holiday in some retired nook in leafy Herefordshire or Shropshire. I had my eye on an old farmhouse at which to make my headquarters for fishing in The Teme, or The Lugg, or The Arrow.

As a boy, I knew that old house well; every corner of it, all the buildings, orchards, and lovely green meadows surrounding it; the woods, the ravines, the far-off mountains, and, above all, the pleasant river which ran through and around the farm, wherein I used to swim and fish for trout and grayling, are vividly before me now.

> " I knew each lane and every alley green,
> Dingle and bushy dell . . . .
> And every bosky bourn from side to side,
> My daily walk and ancient neighbourhood."

But hard and inexorable fate has ordered me off in quite a different direction. All being well, my autumnal holiday will be spent in the Rocky Mountains! If I have called such a fate as that hard, it is only because of the uncertainty of it. A young man, I fancy, would see nothing but delight in it; but for an old man in his seventh decade, and one not accustomed to travel, it is like tearing up his roots and plunging down stream into the unknown.

I am going to fish in the Rockies. I shall

take with me that immaculate tackle which last year inspired me with such hopes in Dovedale. I hear of places where you have only to cast your fly and you pull out a 5 lb. trout (nothing less) with positive certainty; and without taking him off your hook, you have simply to swing him a little behind you into a natural boiling geyser, and in ten minutes your 5-pounder is cooked and ready for your lunch. That is but a small specimen of the kind of sport I am anticipating! That's the sort of thing that inspires me!

But then there is the reverse of this pretty picture, which sometimes, in melancholy moments, makes me contemplate my enforced holiday as a hardship on the part of fate. Are there not mosquitoes on that side of the broad Atlantic? Are there not Red Indians and grizzly bears? I have pictured myself walking though a narrow glen, fishing-rod in hand, in the angler's contemplative mood, and suddenly finding myself confronted by a grizzly! Must, or rather *will*, he retire, or must I? I never fired a revolver in my life, so I should not think of carrying one; besides, I have no thirst for a grizzly's blood, and I

only hope he has none for mine. I am sure
if he will let me alone I won't meddle with
him. Alas! I get a hug and a pat, and my
fate and my fishing are ended!

Then, again, I dream of encountering a
band of black-feet, or crow's feet, or spotted-
tailed Indians, in feathers and war-paint,
armed with tomahawk and scalping-knife. I
yield my hoary, or I may say my bald scalp
to that horrid knife, and *so* my fate is ended.
When I think of things in that way, am I
wrong in talking of it as a *hard* fate? Then
there are six-shooters, bowie-knives, buffaloes,
and rattlesnakes!

Nevertheless, to the Rockies I am bound,
in spite of all such gloomy possibilities. My
passage money is already paid and my berth
secured in the good ship "Cunardia": which
is, I am told, one of the finest vessels afloat;
so I hope I shall be able to give a good
account of her.

My youngest son Frank, who has always
been somewhat of a rolling stone, and to
whom, in the old country, neither wool nor
pelf would stick, is now settled away up at
the foot of the Rocky Mountains; and when

he has sometimes written to me for money, and I have asked him how he has spent it, his answer has invariably been "Come and see!"

Year after year I have put off going, but now I am beginning to feel that if I am ever to go, I must delay no longer; so I am about to see with my own eyes where my money has gone to, and what may be the chances of any portion of it coming back to me.

Frank was always a peculiar youth to manage. He began life in my City counting-house, but he soon tired of it. He had formed the notion that he was better suited to the free life of the prairie than to the routine work of City business. Of course he knew nothing about prairie life, and he would not be persuaded that his notions were but the outcome of a disordered imagination; he was well off where he was, with fair chances before him; but he was quite prepared to throw those chances away, and to strike out into the Far West. He was a strong, healthy, good-looking youth, fond of society, and very popular, and consequently, was gradually being led into habits of extravagance which might have ended badly. I was therefore, willing to humour his wishes.

In the year 1880 I paid his passage to America, and he began his career by engaging himself to a farmer in Minnesota, who for a small stipend was to instruct him in farming and give him his board in exchange for his work.

When Frank began with the farmer, it is not too much to say that he was totally ignorant of everything belonging to a farm; but he had not been on this farm for six months before he became convinced that he had learnt everything there was to learn, and that he could give a few wrinkles to his master.

Then he told me that there was a wonderful farm to be had close at hand, dirt cheap, a chance not to be lost; it was a small place of about 200 acres with good house and building, and splendid feeding prairie-land adjoining. This, he said, was just the place for him to begin on; and he produced such elaborate figures to prove to me that, although the previous occupant had failed there, enormous profits—one hundred per cent. at least—could be made of it, if managed in accordance with his enlightened views, rather than in the humdrum way in which the previous farmer had come to grief. He wrote to me so urgently, so persistently, so enthusiastically, that I, although with many misgivings, found him the money wherewith to purchase and stock the place. More money was expended on that farm than I am now willing to acknowledge, but everything went along swimmingly for a short period.

As time went on things did not seem to thrive so well as was hoped. The corn crop was not up to the mark; the cattle did not fetch the expected price; two or three horses died, and, on the whole, the first year's work had not paid its expenses. But Frank was not disheartened; he wrote courageously home for more money, and worked hard, ploughing and planting, digging and hoeing. I was at least pleased to find him sticking to his work so bravely, and exhibiting no desire to "cave in," although it was evident that his life was a pretty hard one, and his daily fare rough enough.

One day I got a letter from him telling me that he was going to sell the farm, as he had got another scheme in view which would land him in a fortune in a very short time.

The scheme was something quite new in that part of the country, and was a safe success.

The idea was to sell his farm, and with the produce establish a Creamery, for the purpose of buying up all the cream from the farmers for many miles round, and supply all the western cities, and even eastward, as far as New York, with the best butter that could be made, and at prices of hitherto unknown moderation.

Frank supplied me with figures which proved conclusively that after estimating cost of plant, and interest thereon, horses and carts for driving round and collecting, wages of carters and butter-makers, and the prime cost of the cream, the best butter could be produced at a prime cost of sixpence a pound, while the very lowest at which it could possibly be sold was a shilling or 1s. 2d. a pound. This, after making ample allowance for cost of transit, &c., would clearly leave a very handsome profit; the success of the thing was too obvious to be for a moment questioned.

So Frank sold his farm at about what it had originally cost him, but with a total loss of his year's labour, and money sunk in improvements; and went to work in connection with a partner, a practical man, who joined him with no capital, but who, in consideration of his knowledge and experience, was to share equally in the profits, first allowing Frank fair interest for his capital. The local newspapers puffed the new enterprise, and spoke in glowing terms of the pluck and energy of the young Englishman: for a time things looked quite promising.

Frank wrote home with his usual buoyancy and asked for more money to purchase sundry articles and machinery absolutely needed to carry on the rapidly-growing business.

But, alas! for the glowing hopes of youth! At the end of a year it was found by a balance-sheet carefully, and I believe fairly, drawn up by the business partner, that there was nothing left but the plant; the working capital for purchases and expenses was gone. The price of butter had fallen enormously, and the price of cream and cost of collecting it had exceeded the original calculations, whilst the plant, except as a going concern, was not worth much.

It was found necessary either that Frank should put in 2,000 dollars more capital (which he said would set them right), or he must give up the creamery. He did give it up, and was left high and dry to begin the world again with a capital of about two hundred dollars.

I am told that the working partner still carries on the business, and having got hold of the plant at a nominal price, is now really making the thing pay.

But Frank was out of it, and Minnesota was no longer a place for him. With the small capital above mentioned he decided to strike out west for the Rockies.

How he fared I will tell you in my next letter.

LETTER No. II.

Frank's dearly-bought experience—A start for the Rockies—Magnificent scenery—Indian scouts and revolvers—Advice to parents—Frank's determination to "rough it."

London, August, 1885.

I HAVE now given you a short account of how Frank managed to get through his two first years of farming life in Minnesota, and how he (or rather I) was worse off in the end than at the beginning.

He had purchased experience at my expense; his money was nearly all gone, and with what remained he resolved to start off for the Rocky Mountains with a friend. This friend was a young fellow, who had gone out from the City of London fired with the notion that the Great West was the proper place for him, that there was nothing like a life in the open prairie, where a little work would be diversified by a good deal of hunting, shooting, and riding about.

So this youth immediately on his reaching Frank, to whom he had been highly commended by friends at home, borrowed a hundred dollars from him, and they started off together to seek their fortunes in the Rockies.

I think I cannot do better than send you some extracts from Frank's letters, which will give you a fair notion of his progress from the year 1883 to this time, and show, at all events, that amid a good many ups and downs, and hardships of no ordinary character, he has up to this point "stuck to it;" while his friend who accompanied him to the Rockies, suddenly bolted, leaving Frank in the lurch, and minus the money he had lent him. The first letter is dated June, 1883.

"MY DEAR PARENTS,

"I have just struck out here; I had nothing to do at M. The creamery business was finished up, and I can get better pay working out here than there.

I started with S. on Monday, and we arrived here on Thursday, a distance of 1,100 miles, right through the Rockies.

"The view from our window looks out across a valley to the Rocky Mountains, and down the valley for a distance of fifty miles; the scenery is magnificent; the mountains are capped with snow. On Monday we start for a place called Clark's Forks, 120 miles S. W., just north of 'The National Park.' We stage it for sixty miles, and either walk or take ponies the rest, up to a height of 7,000 feet above sea level, to work on some fencing at two and a half dollars a day. There are lots of ways of making a living there, and I hope of saving money. The town here is full of Indian scouts, and every man carries a revolver; in fact, as you may suppose, it is a rough place, and we shall have to look sharp after ourselves with our revolvers. Bears (grizzlies) are thick in the district we are going to, also antelope, deer, and Indians. . . . . We are in the roughest of countries, but I am determined to fight my way through, and in the end I hope to come out successful. . . .

"My motive in coming here is simply to work hard and save money. If any thing should happen to either of us you will hear from one of us; we go with our lives in our hands.

"As we are green hands just yet, we only get two dollars, but after a little while we are to get three dollars a day.

"I have now just money enough to get to our destination."

Notwithstanding the fact that this boy had been losing my money all the time, I did not feel altogether disheartened; for I had found him as candid about his failures as he had been sanguine about his successes, and he always gave me sufficiently clear accounts as to *how* the money had gone. I was pleased with the pluck he had shown under difficulties from which many a young fellow would have shrunk.

I had found out by this time that I had acted very unwisely in supplying an inexperienced youth, however energetic and right principled, with capital to start farming in a new country without any practical knowledge whatever.

Hundreds of youths go out to America and the Colonies every year under circumstances very like those of my son. Indulgent parents supply them with money at once to start them in life in an occupation to which they bring nothing but conceit and ignorance combined, and their money is as certain to be lost as if it were thrown into the sea.

My advice to parents situated similarly to myself is never to give an unlimited supply of money to start with. Allow your son just so much as will keep him from starvation, and let him work out his luxuries for himself. Let him rough it for three or four years at least; by that time he will have discovered how far his boyish dreams have been realized by experience, and he will have shown the stuff he is made of. He will either have succumbed and gone home, or broken down in some more disastrous way, or he will have gained experience which may justify his starting in business with some hope of his being able to take care of himself and his money, and to pull through.

My son had gained experience at my expense, and now I decided that he should gain a little more at his own cost. I thought it better that he should rough it for himself, and this he had made up his mind to do.

LETTER No. III.

A hundred and twenty miles' walk—Axe, pick-axe, and shovel—A four-hundred-feet roll down the mountain—Rough living—An Indian scare—Deadly fumes—Working round a smelter—Fishing in Lake "Abundance"—Disturbed by a grizzly.

London, August, 1885.

I PROPOSE now to occupy a few pages with extracts from Frank's letters, which will give a fair notion of his progress up to the time of my sailing, and from that point I purpose to give you an account of my own adventures.

In his next letter, which is dated Cook's City, July 6, 1883, he says :—

"I started out from Minnesota, as there was nothing for me to do there that would pay me so well. . . . .

We walked from Bozeman, 120 miles through the Rockies, with a promise of work, but the roads and creeks, or rather mountain torrents, which we had to cross are so bad at present that the smelter cannot be got up here yet, and so we are employing ourselves in building a log cabin for the winter for ourselves. The trouble is that winter will soon be here . . . and as I paid all S.'s expenses as well as my own, besides lending him 100 dollars, I am afraid I shall not have much left. . . . We are now 120 miles from the nearest neighbourhood, right in the heart of the Rockies, so that letters are scarce and far between. From Bozeman (where Mrs. Blackmore was buried) the carrier comes once a week, but in winter, I suppose, once a fortnight.

"The scenery here is magnificent; we are now in a gulch, with a range of mountains on each side of us; a small camp composed of log cabins, at present about fifty people, but a boom is expected, and we shall share it. We have already taken up a lot, which costs nothing, and are building a log cabin, which in two weeks we hope to finish. . . . We hope in winter to save by getting an elk or two, of which there are plenty, also bears, mountain lions, &c. The air is very fine and rare here, and happens to agree with us both."

"*Clark's Fork, August* 5, 1883.

"When we first came here (on foot, 120 miles from Bozeman) we were promised work, but on account of a misunderstanding between our employers, we had to wait a few days; however, we have both been working on a mountain pass, at two dollars and board

WOODCHOPPER'S CABIN, FROM FRANK'S SKETCH.

a day. The work, swinging an axe, pick-axe, and shovel, is not so very hard, but the sleeping out in the open under our two blankets, sometimes pouring with rain, was not very clever. There were about twenty of us and a black cook, and the amount of bluebottle flies and other insects I have eaten would have turned my stomach but for having a marvellous appetite.

"Boiled elk, bear, and tea was the programme for two weeks. When the job was finished, we immediately got work fixing up and shovelling charcoal round a smelter at three dollars, *without* board; so we are now working at it, and come home at noon for our dinner in a little shack near the smelter; hours, seven to twelve; one to six. We cook our bread when we get through at six, generally boiling some buffalo meat for our next day's supply.

"I must not forget to mention that our appearance at night is somewhat similar to a coalheaver's.

"This is good, honest, though dirty work. Our intention at present is to save up 100 dollars, start off from here, and camp up at Bridger's, 130 miles from here (about twelve miles on the other side of Bozeman), and cut cordwood to supply Bozeman, and by hard work hope to make 1,000 dollars by next July. . . . . I want you to think that I am doing my very best to make and save money. We have not had even potatoes for a month. Goods are too expensive here, as they have to be hauled from Bozeman.

"Before we went on to the road business we had a three days' job about five miles away, up on the side of a mountain covered with snow, and had to pack our blankets, grub, &c., across the snow, making sure of our footsteps, otherwise it might have been all up with us. Once we did slip, and went flying down the mountain for 400 feet; but there happened to be a curve which pulled us up. I shall never forget the

AN AWKWARD ROLL.

sensation. We tried to get a horse across. He slipped, rolled over and over with our blankets, frying pan, and all on his back. We thought it was all over with him, but he got up after tumbling down 300 feet, shook himself, and walked off, leaving our teapot smashed in. I believe the old beast had been there before."

"*August* 19, 1883.

". . . As long as my health keeps up I don't care. I can get along well; but this high altitude and the rough living, nothing but bread and elk meat, which is liable to give one dysentery, has stopped me working two or three days. However, I hope to be all right to-morrow.

"I have been working round a smelter (which has not yet actually begun to work) from seven o'clock to six, at three dollars a day, without board, so that, though I don't spend a cent except for meat, sugar, flour, and coffee, which, by the way, are frightfully dear, having to be hauled 120 miles, I cannot save much. . . . This is the roughest of lives, but as I can get good wages I can put up with it.

"My idea now is to work on as long as possible here. The smelter is run by water power, and when it freezes up work will stop. Then either go to a place near Bozeman and cut wood, or hire out somewhere else; and when the winter is through make my way out to Washington territory as soon as the snow will allow; take up a homestead claim somewhere the other side of the Columbia River, work in a lumber camp all the winter, and work the farm in the summer. . . . . There was an Indian scare in camp last night. Ten Indians turned up fully armed, but they were only after some of their horses the whites had stolen;

two men were arrested, but one escaped, tearing away with a horse and six-shooter at full gallop."

"*August* 26, 1883.

". . . I can now fully appreciate the value of money, having worked hard for it lately. The 'boom' I mentioned meant simply that we staked out ground near town, built a log foundation on it (to hold it by homestead right), so that should this mining town turn out another Leadville, the lot would be valuable, though it did not cost a cent save our two days' labour. . . . You also mention that I said I was going to get 20 dollars a week. So I did, but have had to lay off two days, and still have plenty of money in hand ; but laying off when work shuts down cannot be helped. Last night, for instance, I worked from seven o'clock to seven in the morning in the smelter here for 14*s*. at carrying bullion (silver and lead, 100 lbs. weight), but I am afraid I cannot work again to-night, as my feet are blistered and dried up. Besides, the fumes, which are deadly, have rather upset me. Though the wages are good, the risk is too great. Out of the 14*s*. (three and a half dollars) I have to pay 2*s*. a meal for board, as one has to live a little better than 'baching it' at this sort of work.

"Milk is a *necessity*, and at 1*s*. 6*d*. a quart runs away with money. I must not forget to mention that there is a fearful rush for the four cows owned by an old rancher here, whose *spring* is by far too handy.

"I would have sent you a little sketch, but the principal mixer of my oil colours is missing, and 120 miles too far to send. . . . Winter is fast coming on, and the snow lies from five to seven inches deep on the level, outside work being nearly shut off.

"S. left here two days ago to work on a ranche, and I am not very sorry for it, as he would neither save nor try and push along; so at present I am without a partner in this wild life.

"In my last I told you I was not feeling very well, so I went up on the mountains from the valley to Lake 'Abundance,' and I send you herewith a short account of my excursion. . . . I am sorry to say that churches are out of the question here. The old miners are a perfectly godless set, and if they were to catch sight of what they call a 'sky pilot' he would swing."

"FISHING AMONG THE ROCKY MOUNTAINS.

"Just a line to tell you of a little fishing expedition that I went on with a friend. We started from here, Cook's City (? city, there are only a few log cabins), at daybreak on one of those mornings only known to early risers, cool, with slight delicious breezes fanning the valley of pines. We took with us a pack-horse to carry our blankets, grub, &c., and I must here mention that a man soon learns to pack, there being very little both as to quantity and size—two blankets each, ten pounds of flour, coffee, bacon, frying-pan, and coffee-pot completing the outfit.

"Our way took us over a steep mountain leading through forests, down again to a long plateau with a rushing torrent as its centre, until we again ascended to a high divide or rocky ridge, whence we caught sight of our lake, some four miles distant, shut in between the bases of surrounding mountains.

"I must not forget the charming view we had from the divide. Far away for the distance of quite eighty miles could be seen mountain after mountain rising in the clear, though mighty rare, atmosphere, some looking like ancient castles, others as flat as tables, all bare and rugged from above timber line. After a pipe and look to the trappings of our pack-saddle, we started to descend, and camped within a mile of the lake, near a creek of clear snow water. A breakfast the next morning of bacon, coffee, and bread cooked in frying-pan, at the cooking of which I am quite an expert, and we started for the lake, catching grasshoppers on our way before the sun had made them shed their overcoats and get too lively.

"The first throw I made was with a piece of red flannel, and hooked three nice salmon trout in no time, weighing from a pound to two and a half; but they seemed as the morning advanced to fight shy of such indigestible stuff as flannel, and I treated them to some nice hoppers of a brownish tint, catching eight more. The hoppers went wrong after a little, and I was hard up for a new bait, when, happening to nearly land another fish, I pulled a piece of his jaw (do you anglers call it the jaw?) out, threw again with this, and caught two more; it was a small piece of the white gristly flesh, and wriggled like a worm in the water. Time for grub came on: we started a fire, fried some fish, ate it, smoked, of course, and I think went to sleep—I know I did ; when my friend roused me up and told me to listen, and sure enough we could hear an old bear rolling rocks on the other side of the lake, some quarter of a mile distant. Both of us started with our rifles to have a shot, though, if within fifty yards and the shot is not fatal (and bears have been shot three times through the heart, and yet not killed), it is all up with you ; if near a tree, up you go.

"However, we did not see the bruin, and perhaps it was lucky for us we did not, as the older the hunters, the more cautious and wary they are about these enormously strong brutes. Let me tell of my first bear story out here. We were then down at the mill creek, some eighty miles distant, when we met three hunters, who the night before had met a bear. They came upon her unawares, each discharging his Winchester, though only one slightly wounded her. She made a rush for the nearest of them, and then for a scatter—one jumped into a creek running fast enough to carry him off his legs ; the other climbed up a tree, which, being rotten, fell with a crash. However, they all escaped, and lucky for them, as the strength and agility of these Rocky Mountain bears is marvellous ; they can lift and roll about boulders of six hundred pounds, and tear up young trees from the ground in a surprising manner. To return to our fishing, we had good sport also the next day, catching forty-two ; and on our nearing the lake saw two young elk. My friend fired, but missed, I having left my gun behind.

"As our mail carrier starts early to-morrow, I must conclude, and, should you want any information as to species of fish with their anatomical peculiarities, I will try and find them out and send you.—I am, &c.,

"F.

"*Cook's City, Montana, August* 30, 1883."

LETTER No. IV.

Starting afresh on a new farm—Wheat forty to seventy-five bushels to the acre—Felling trees and fencing "Life here is deuced hard"—Somewhat despondent—Forty below zero—Ink and bacon frozen—Anxiety for General Gordon—Working in snow up to the waist.

London, August 15, 1885.

IN September, 1883, Frank worked his way back into the more civilized regions of Montana, and with his usual enthusiasm he wrote to me :—

"This is the best country I have yet struck, and I am sure that I shall do well here. My idea now is to hack up 160 acres, get a team, wagon, and horses, build a small house, plough forty acres this fall, put it into wheat, and ten acres of oats ; . . . if *I only had the start now which I had when I went to Minnesota my fortune would soon be made I feel sure.* Wheat goes from forty to even seventy-five bushels to the acre, and at 4*s.* a bushel, one ought to make plenty of money. A member of Parliament and several English gentlemen have lately visited this valley, and were surprised at the fertility of the soil. If a little later on you could send me some money to start with again, it will help me to get a home, and so far as I can see pave my way to a large thing.

"By chance I have run out a piece of land where I can secure the entire water right for a farm. I cannot see any thing but success before me. . . . I am going to work out with the team every day I can spare from the farm and earn money. . . . I would not ask you for a cent if I could possibly help it, and I only want you to think I am doing the very best for myself. I don't spend any money at all but what is absolutely necessary, and I must beg you to give me another small start to put me on my legs again.

"I worked on the thresher here two days ago, and the wheat on the farm I worked went forty-three bushels to the acre. On some stalks two heads; this is a second crop on same land and no manure."

The result of these appeals was that I supplied Frank with some more money, and he purchased the farm and other things partly on credit (at a ruinous interest), partly with his own savings, and partly with the cash I sent him.

In October of the same year (1883) he wrote —

"I have got my cabin up and ploughed up some land, and have these last five days been hauling logs down from the mountain to build my stable, and, in

FRANK'S CABIN, FROM A SKETCH BY HIMSELF.

fact, have come to town to have my log chain mended. . . .

"Don't imagine I am having a good time and spending money for the sake of spending. I am up long before daylight and working hard until dark. This winter I hope to get out 600 posts, and fencing for the farm, besides working round to earn money. I bought fifteen bushels of seed wheat at one dollar, and sowed and harrowed it in my neighbour's piece of breaking.

This is called 'renting;' I receive two-thirds of the crop and he gets one-third. As I was not on my land in time to plough enough, this gives me a share in the winter wheat crop, and next year I hope to put in twenty acres of wheat and five of potatoes."

In December, 1883, he wrote to his brother :

"A letter from you now and again would do no positive injury to either party ; send me a line when you can, as I don't expect to be home for some years, and I do not want to lose track of any of you. Many thanks for papers, send me any old magazines you can. I read for company's sake, as I am all alone here, and don't want to forget how to read.

"The life here is deuced hard, but I feel certain of reaping a good harvest, and am going to stick to it. At present I am working about two miles from home, cutting down trees for fencing. I then start them down the mountain on a small natural quelch on the snow ; they go like greased lightning, and make a terrible noise, which is echoed and re-echoed through the mountains.

"I have just completed my stable which looks *boss*, logs with mud chinking ; next year I intend putting in twenty acres of spring wheat. . . . As I have just bought some beef-bones I am making a fine stew ; which makes my little kitten mew and skip round, being the first taste for her little sides."

"*Jan.* 1, 1884.

"I wanted, if possible, to begin the new year without having to write for money, but I am now having the hardest time I have ever had; weather excessively cold, and very little grub in the house. . . . I don't like to give up my best hopes, so if you can let me have the little balance I mentioned, it would make me even. . . . It was indeed a quiet Christmas for me, at work in the woods at my fencing; and now comes new year, just the same."

"*A few days later.*

"Sometimes I begin to despair, as the undertaking I have gone into requires more money than I really thought it would. . . . Don't think by this that I am getting discouraged with the work or prospects—far from it. . . . It seems to me that I cannot start to write a letter unless I make some allusion to money, but I am so anxious to get straightened up that I cannot help it. . . . The money has wholly been expended on the ranche, no folly or stupidities have been indulged in, and I feel fully competent to take care of anything I get now. . . . Winter has set in now nearly two months, and those who *can*, keep near the stoves. Every day is much the same to me, and all I hope is, that I don't get hurt, or become ill, as getting out timber alone is dangerous work; snow slides, bringing rocks and timber along, may occur at any moment.

" . . . Time is creeping along, and spring not far off, bringing back the horrid grizzlies and panthers."

"*Jan.* 10, 1884.

"I am obliged to write in pencil, as my ink has frozen, and adding water to it has taken away nearly all its colour. The snow is nearly three feet deep on the level, making it mighty hard work to get about; however, if it lets up it will make it all the better sleighing. I am still at work in the woods chopping; up to my waist in snow, getting down fencing and firewood; uncomfortable. Though when I have a good soup and get a refreshing sleep I forget all the discomforts. If it snows to-morrow I shall plaster up my shack inside, having bought a bushel of lime. . . . Every day I learn something new, and expect to do so for years to come. I look forward to a bright future. All farming operations have ceased long ago, and nothing can be done until the spring.

" . . . I have made several friends out here, but have been very careful who they were, and sometimes by moonlight I skip away five miles and have a chat with a good old timer. . . . My paint box has not come from Cook City yet; when it does I will try my hand at giving you some faint idea of this superb scenery."

"*Feb.* 8, 1884.

" I told you that S. had disappeared altogether, and with him my hundred dollars and other money he owed me. Young B. has now come out here, and has so far joined me that we go halves in expenses, and he helps me in all work. . . . The weather the last four days has been intensely cold, forty below zero. In fact, so cold, that we dared not go out to work, and though we have just put a floor in the shack, just in time, at night the cold wakes one up and sends the creeps down one's back. Our bacon freezes solid, saw and axe only having any effect. Is there no old aunt to die and leave me some money? I do hate to be always bothering you. . . Of course we 'bache it' here, and as there is no great variety to cook, cooking is no great hardship.

"We have just finished our supper of bacon and beans, and some stray pieces of meat; and as Burnaby says in his book that *tea* stays longer by one than coffee, we have been *teaing* for some time.

"Now is the dull season, of course; but we are getting a few hens, hoping the weather will improve, to make them cackle. It does not seem like the same place now I have some one with me—much pleasanter and a great help in working.

"I must not forget to mention that I hurt my back a few days ago lifting some logs, and I get up every morning like an old man; however, B. has put a porous plaister on my back, and I really don't know which is the greater nuisance of the two, back-ache or plaister."

"*March* 5, 1884.

"Thanks for sending me the papers! I really don't know what we would do without them; the neighbours make regular calls, weather permitting, to borrow them. Our anxiety for General Gordon is as great here as I suppose it is with you. . . . Although life is hard and rough here, I like it more and more, and I trust to do well here: our plans for next year are as follows:—To put in about four acres of garden produce, onions, potatoes, &c., and sell the produce; and if we have luck we shall do well on this; not to put any crop in at all, as machinery is too expensive; a reaper, rake and thrashing expenses would eat up our profits, especially as the machinery would have to be bought on time, a system I am not going in for if I can help it. To fence the whole 160 acres in, the posts for which I have already cut (640), besides hen-house logs, &c., with barbed wire, will cost £23, but I hope to sell hay enough off the place to cover this. When the fencing is done, I shall start out somewhere to get work, and stay away six months (the law allows this under the Homestead Act), and B. will run the ranche.

"I hope to earn three dollars a day, but cannot figure on it, as all sorts of accidents may happen; I might not get paid, or I may hurt myself in some way. B. has already six cows from which we hope to make butter and raise the calves; this is the best and surest business, they increase rapidly. The natural grass (bunch grass) is not only good feed, but strengthening and fattening. . . .

"During the season B. ought to have time to cut up at least fifty cords of wood, which left to the fall to season, readily brings in Bozeman six dollars a cord, or in all, 300 dollars. . . . As the 'Rheumatiz' has got a slight hold of me, the result of working in the snow up to my waist after fencing and timber, I must make an early start to bed. . . . A general thaw was followed last night by eight inches of snow, bringing the average up again to two feet ten inches on the level."

LETTER No. V.

Never had such a hard time—Camping out in the Rockies—Horses decamp—Left in the lurch—A terrible fright—Crossing a torrent—"Old Jim" taking a roll—Pack smashed—"Old Jim" in a snow-drift—Woke up by a grizzly—What the newspapers said of it—Cutting fencing poles in the snow—Christmas Day—Pickles and plum pudding—The consequences—A dance—Cowboys and farmers' daughters—"Shall I turn tail?"—A profitable old cow—The nicest little ranche in Montana—Start on a sheep drive 300 miles—"The healthiest place I ever struck."

London, August 20, 1885.

N the following May, 1884, he wrote: "I never had such a hard time of it in my life." And in September to his brother:—

". . . The truth is, I have been some seventy

miles away from home, and shall be gone again in a few days to look for a winter job. The new railway has knocked things topsy-turvy.

"Labour, when I first came here, was scarce, and well paid for, but now things are very dull here. However, there is a good prospect for better things. They all say that one railroad spoils a town, two bring it to par again, and three make it 'boom.' This seems the general rule throughout America. On my way out to the mountains after work, some three months back, I found a good prospect for copper, and since then we have taken up four distinct veins in the centre of a good mining camp; but we shall simply represent them each year to hold them so that it will not ruin us. (Representation is ten days' work each year on the mine for five years, then you can get your patent.) We may make a fortune from them, and we may not make a cent. However, we shall not let it interfere with our work. I could send one of your papers a decent article—'A Prospector's Life, or Hunting after Gold.' The newspapers come in mighty handy, and are read through and through.

"CAMPING OUT IN THE ROCKIES.

"Let me give you a short account of my little trip. Starting from my log cabin early in the spring, when the snow was still in drifts, in places fifteen feet deep, I made my way some seventy miles into the mountains. I had a little Indian pony, and a horse old enough in tricks, if not in years, to carry my pack, consisting of my blankets, tent, and grub. Grub!

why, certainly. Fifty pounds of flour, a tin of self-raising flour, labelled 'absolutely pure' of course, (a lawsuit ought to follow up this libel,) two pounds of coffee, salt, frying-pan, cup, and a well-stocked box of matches. The above was to last me a month or more. I am forgetting the bacon. The day I set out was beautifully clear, and my journey progressed through ever-changing scenery. Before me and on each side were the snow-capped mountains, still white as they had been for six months past, and fringed along their sides by a massive belt of timber, at the foot of which my little pony and old carcase ahead were picking their way, treading lightly lest their weight should precipitate them through the hardened crust of snow.

"Looking back, I could see my little home nestled close against the mountains, and I fancied, too, that I could see my little kitten on the roof, perhaps mourning its late master, or more probably lamenting its cosy bed inside. I stayed but a short time to contemplate this scene, a fairer could not be found—a beautiful valley, surrounded on all sides by high-towering mountains of every shape and form. Three brooks teeming with trout wend their headlong way; I say headlong, for they rise from the very top of yon snowy peaks, and come tearing and roaring down at this season of the year, when the sun is getting the better of the snow, and feeding these streams, which eventually fall into the flowing Missouri.

"Continuing my journey for a short time, my ponies wanted to stop for a feed, and I felt the same inclination ; so I unpacked, scratched a fire together, made some coffee, and while my gentle steeds were pawing and nibbling at grass in bare places, took to my pipe of 'Wills' Westward Ho' (supposed to be) tobacco, dried and cut fine, but it ought to be labelled 'Old Boot Tops,' instead of 'Uncle Sam.' So absorbed was I in my pipe, I did not notice that my Arabs had decamped, leaving me in the lurch. Ascending a higher point, I could just distinguish them a mile off, and had it not been for the snow, they would have been five miles away, making steadily for home, though why they wanted to go there I do not know. Certainly not for food ; at least, I could very rarely find any luxuries there myself. A brisk walk, with much shouting, 'Whoa ! where are you off to?' &c., brought me up to them. A hasty return, quickened by prodigious cudgellings, though my pack-horse has a hide like a rhinoceros, packing up, and giving old Jim a happy reminder, I again rode along. Towards evening it became excessively chilly. I had taken a little *eau de vie* with me, which, however, I always put in my pack, as its immediate presence on my person might tempt me too often; so starting my pony at a little quicker pace, and getting off, I made for old Jim, just a little ahead of me ; but no sooner was I within reach of the old boy's tail than he started off at a brisk gambol. Nothing would induce him to stop till he had left me some distance behind. However, being persistent, and by making little detours, I secured him and the bottle.

"The place to which I was bound was some seventy

miles from home, and through a rough and wild country, infested with bears, mountain lions, and wolves. The weather at night was very cold, and my fare not princely. At sundown I struck off into the timber, lighted my camp fire, secured one of the horses, and in a short time was fast asleep, dreaming of delightful trips by land or sea. Let me not forget a little incident which occurred this first night. It being a calm evening, the wind having lulled, before retiring for the night I did not put up my little tent. At somewhere between midnight and three o'clock I was awakened by a terrible (or it seemed so then) howl close to my head, which had got out of the blankets, and on looking up I saw an awful head not a foot from mine, teeth, jaws, and ears. It did not take as long as it does to recount to find my head where my toes were; I had performed a sort of double somersault, landing me in the snow, and then I looked back and found the terrible monster who was ready to devour me was off at a two-forty pace in the opposite direction. After all, it was only old 'Jim.' He must have been scared at a coyote (wolf) or other marauder, and sought my protection; but he was certainly scared far worse the second time. Shaking off the snow, and having another pipe between the blankets just to consider awhile as to whether the old animal was not going to cause me more trouble, I soon fell asleep again, dreaming of bears, tigers, and every other household pet.

"On waking, my blankets seemed heavier than on going to bed. It had snowed during the early hours, and they were converted into white ermine. One more snooze, and then to get up, shake my blankets, light my fire; breakfast through, and horses saddled, away I start to commence my second day. A few hours after starting I lost sight of the valley I had come from, but in front of me again was one of the finest panoramas I had ever seen. From my elevated position, and for a distance of fifty miles at least, I could see mountain after mountain towering one above another—high, sharp, rocky peaks, and undulating table-lands. Leaving this, I broke off down a narrow divide or cañon, wending my way towards a bright stream, near which I could discern a small house, some fencing, and cattle ranging around.

"Two hours' ride brought me to the little stream, now a raging torrent. The farmer shouted to me not to attempt the crossing, but my motto is 'Excelsior.' I had terrible hard work to cross.

"'Try not the pass!' the old man said,
'Dark lowers the tempest overhead.
The roaring torrent is deep and wide.'

"My horses were very nearly carried away down the rushing stream. However, we succeeded at last; and a warm fire and a chat with a human being, for it seemed a month since starting, revived my hopes. I found the house to be owned by a cattle-man whom I met just before entering, ready saddled, and on his way to hunt up some game. The house is beautifully situated; the stream furnishes an abundant supply of fine mountain trout, many of which have been caught in a little irrigating ditch, which the rancher has run out from the stream to water his garden, and not having time to put them back in the stream, and time to eat them, I presume he prefers the latter. Here, 'midst the heart of the Rockies, lives a man and his wife all alone, not seeing a human being for a month at a time, perfectly happy and healthy, letting their cattle range on the vast undulating lowlands; and here, owing to the amount of wind in winter, they feed all the year round, bare places being thus kept open. Although a pressing invitation was given me to stay, I still journeyed on, following the creek along, and having to cross it no less than nine times until the route indicated to me took up a rough and dry cañon, where, I have since found out, the gentle rattlesnake 'loves to lie a-basking in the sun.' Nothing happened worthy of mention, save old Jim, who, wanting to give his old back (made at an angle of forty-five degrees) a scratch, coolly—I may here use the word, as it was in the snow—squatted down and commenced to roll with my precious pack on his back. My coffee-pot was crushed square, frying-pan jammed into the hunch of bacon, and *eau de vie* bottle smashed. What did I say? Never mind. At length we got to what seemed to me an impassable barrier, a terribly deep snow-drift. If I had reached this place early in the morning all would have been well, but now the sun had softened the upper crust, and the first step old Jim took was up to his neck, his poor old front legs and nose were hidden altogether, presenting a comical picture which I should like to give you a sketch of. Unpacking him, letting him struggle backwards, carrying the pack by pieces nearly a half mile, and letting the horses swim rather than walk through, took me two good hours at least,

OLD JIM IN A SNOW-DRIFT.

landing me on a bare place, only to find that I had another drift almost as bad to go through. A repetition of the above landed me near two or three scattered pines, not knowing in the least where I was or which way to turn, my clothes wet, everything wet, bottle gone, and generally played out.

"I soon made my camp, pitched my tent, heaped up all the wood I could find, and then sat down to brood over my folly in not waiting until a month later, or indeed in making such a risky journey at all. After awhile I was surprised to see, coming evidently from the opposite direction from which I had come, a man with two horses. This, at least, was a blessing, for were he white or black man he should answer me, and tell me all he knew concerning the route.

"He turned out to be a miner returning from a camp through which I had to go, but as he was too anxious to get on, I kindly asked him if he would not take a drink, when suddenly I remembered the smashed bottle. Ample excuses and convincing ones, as he had to go through the same drift, and would there see the mangled remains of my dead soldier ; so we parted, he to continue his journey, and I to bed, though yet only sundown.

"The next morning found me up early, only too anxious to get away from this land of desolation. The preceding evening had landed me on a bare knoll, and a slight wind having sprung up during the night and obliterated the tracks of my unexpected visitor, I had to make my way as well as I possibly could ; old Jim now up and now down, digging him out, unpacking and wearying along, passed the day, and found me camped alongside a creek surrounded by heavy brush.

"It would have been hard to have awoke me when

I did get to sleep, as I had had a fairly rough day of it; still it could not have been more than three hours after I had gone to sleep when I was awoke by a horrible grunting, and the bushes round the tent were

"IT WAS A FINE OLD BRUIN!"

torn and smashed round as if a young cyclone was at work. It could not be old Jim this time; oh, no! it was a fine old bruin! so, hastily putting on my pants, and at the same time giving a terrific yell, feeling for my rifle, which, by the way, I had left at home, and skipping out of the tent, took a very short space of time. As it was now pitch dark, and plenty of roots of trees to run against and tumble over, I had to pull up and listen, and I soon heard with satisfaction the noise some distance past my tent. I evidently had either scared him or he had gone to the tent, taken my bacon, and walked off. Though not fifty yards off, I had a good deal of trouble to find my tent again, and, when found, lay me down, but not to sleep, for awhile at least, until I could hear no more groanings. Old bear-hunters since tell me that he would have done no harm if he had intruded into my tent; if I had feigned being dead he would only have nosed me round and given me a parting slap for old acquaintance' sake, breaking one or two ribs. I think here again discretion was better than valour. The funny part comes later on. Next day I met two prospectors, and told them about the bear. They told it in Bozeman, and next day it is in the paper, reading as follows :—

"'A man out prospecting was aroused from his midnight slumbers by a bear. The night being dark, and no ammunition at hand, he beat a hasty retreat, running two miles, falling into a creek, and then down a deep gully (fortunately sustaining no injuries) in but very scanty clothing; staying out all night, and on returning in the morning, he found his bacon and grub all gone,' &c.

"So much for newspaper reports! I have had several gentle surprises since. I hope to do well in time, and do not expect to return home until I have made a good stake.

"The remainder of my journey passed without further incident."

"*December* 10, 1884.

"Why don't you send me a coloured plate now and then? People in my low scale of life would hang it up on the wall in place of a Millais. . . .

"I can do well here. It is only a question of time, as I have before said. If business were more flourishing, the prices would be better, and this can only be remedied by time. 'Everything comes to him who waits.'

"I am now getting out fencing poles, both for myself and to sell. It is terribly hard work. A walk of three miles, completely up grade, brings me to the top of the mountain range, back of the cabin, and here I cut them on the now already six inches of snow, work them down a 'shoot,' then haul them home on a sleigh. To-day I cut one hundred, and put them in position with my others (three hundred already cut). This may seem easy work, but in reality it is very hard. Even if it snows a foot or two to-morrow, I must still stick to it. I want about one thousand five hundred (a thousand to sell at fourpence a-piece), and it will keep me rushing to do it. What with climbing up and slipping down, cutting and clearing the shoot each fresh snow, walking home again, you may imagine I get pretty fagged out by the end of the day.

"If we had not had such bad luck this summer we (B. and myself) would have been some hundreds of dollars ahead this winter ; but the cattle breaking my garden fence down, and destroying the whole of the garden stuff, and not getting paid for work, it put me a way behind, besides the loss of one of my horses. . . .

"My mule was looking poor when B. came. So we thought to trade him off, and we exchanged him for a pony, and then exchanged the pony for a mare (a good trade). Unfortunately, I lost the mare, but may still get her back next summer ; so I had to get another horse, for which I gave eighty-five dollars. . . . The money you sent me helped to pay for my former team, wagon, harness, tools, and furniture. Though not elaborate, still it all mounted up.

". . . This winter I shall earn all I can, though it is terribly hard to make much this time of year. Boots (rubber) are continually wearing out, and socks too ; my heels are like boards.

"I have come to the conclusion I could learn some language, living or dead, these long winter evenings, if you would send me some books. I read continually of an evening. . . . Wishing you all a merry Christmas and happy new year."

"*December* 31, 1884.

"Since I last wrote we have had a terrible fall of snow, but now all is clear again ; that is to say, the tracks are all broken ; good sleighing and sharp, cold weather. Can you realise 47° below zero? We had this for a day and a half, and it kept us pretty close to the stove.

"B. calculates to buy a piece of railroad land adjoining my ranche, and we can then fence together. . . . He can still live with me, and we can work and help one another. The longer I stay here, the more I like the life. . . . Cattle grow at a surprising pace here. My neighbour, a mile north, sold ten steers at forty dollars a head, for which he was only offered twenty dollars last spring. Thank all round for Christmas cards.

"The hardest thing to do now is to keep warm, and much as we try with patent socks, running round, eating fat bacon, &c., the cold will creep to our toes. . . . A bottle of Crosse and Blackwell's pickles, mixed with a little plum pudding of my own making, we had on Christmas Day, quite made me ill for the time being; however, a dose of horse specific soon put me right again. I really believe the sight of a mince pie would turn my stomach. Life here is without any of the festivities of Old England. If there is a dance, you invite your lady love to go with you, and pay two dollars for the privilege of dancing in a little cabin no bigger than mine (seventeen by nineteen), crowded with cowboys and farmers' daughters. As I have no lady love, nor the money to throw away, I have not given them the pleasure of my society yet.

"Sister A. ought to come out and keep my house for me next summer. Tell her I will build an addition to the mansion if she will come. The mountain air will do her good."

"*March* 14, 1885.

"I have been expecting to hear from you, I may say, very anxiously. . . . *Any* letter would be better than none at all. I feel it all the more here, as I have been doing my very best to get ahead. I am still convinced that I can do well here if I can once get ahead. A little bunch of stock, and my debts cleared, and I can then go right ahead. . . . To-day is my birthday. By next year, if I live, I shall be grey-headed. Snow still a foot deep, though disappearing."

"*May* 17, 1885.

"We are now in full swing of spring work; grass, trees, and my garden are pushing ahead wonderfully. The season is short here, so vegetation has to hurry up to take advantage of the time. . . . I verily believe I got the last piece of Government land in the valley worth taking up with good grass on it, and water running through, but it is too rocky to plough any extent of it. Thirty acres are the most I could work, but as pasturage it will be worth considerable some day.

"I am now in such a position that I hardly know how to look ahead. I have my ranche, which still requires considerable fencing, and ought to be done this spring, as grass is getting scarce, and the stock not only eat it off, but tread it out, so that I ought to take advantage of this spring to get it completely under fence. This, of course, costs money. The barbed wire has to be bought. I have already a good deal up, besides the 1,350 poles and 640 posts that I cut and put up myself. All this takes time, of course, and prevents my working out anywhere in the mountains.

"Now the question is, What am I to do? I still owe — dollars. I hardly like to say that I had better turn tail and come home, or get a berth, if possible, in New York or somewhere. This is not my wish at all. In truth, I would sooner stay and work on here. I like the country immensely, and, with the aid of capital, can do well; but, on the other hand, I can only go on as a day labourer, earning enough, perhaps, this summer and winter to pay my debts, which are piling up at a cent and a half a month interest (18 *per cent.*). Of course, you will take into account my early failure in Minnesota; but though I know it was my own fault, I put it down to a run of bad luck and want of experience. I assure you I have done nothing but work since I have been out here, building up my home, and looking out for a job as the chances came. . . . My debts paid and clear here, I can, of course, make a living, but I want to do something more than that.

"If you cannot possibly give me the necessary start, I must go off and wander round from month to month. It seems to me that I have done nothing but have money since I left England, but since the first loss it has come in in rather small sums, that have been swallowed up in odds and ends about the place.

"You need not think me grumbling or grasping. I long to get a fair, clear start, and have done with it.

Whatever you do, do not think I am tired or want a change. The more I see of this life the more I like it.

"My *Homestead Right*[1] lasts for five years, and until they have expired I cannot get a title from the Government for my land, so that I am not likely to throw up my work and right without a good cause. . . .

"*P.S.—A trip out here would do you good, and you could see for yourself how things stand.*"

"*June* 26, 1885.

". . . You ask me whether my ranche does not produce anything—have I no cattle to sell, &c. If you refer to my letters, you will see that I mentioned having bought an old cow cheap (for £4), which gave us milk last winter, but as she was a little too decrepit to raise a calf, I traded her off this spring for a little mare, which, again, I sold for 200 cedar posts, worth twenty cents apiece, or forty dollars. Thus my old cow, which I gave £4 for, will, when the posts are delivered and sold, bring me in £8. (As the spring has been unusually wet, the man has not come up to time with the posts, but I shall have them shortly.) My garden ought to bring me in £20. I have the finest set of cabbages, peas, and potatoes in the valley, my team, and this spring I have 130 chickens, 100 of which we raised this spring, and more are hatching out now. Twenty-five acres broken ready for a crop of wheat that is ready to sow by September, and one mile and a half of fence, or 150 acres, enclosed. In addition to this, I have just finished putting up a little

[1] See Appendix.

milk house on the creek, and am terribly proud of it; it looks like a Swiss châlet, gabled ends, &c. I am all the more proud of it, as I have hewed the logs and put it up at odd times of an evening. By next autumn, when I hope to have everything complete, I shall have, if not the prettiest, at least one of the nicest little ranches in Montana, magnificent building spot, icy cold water all the year round, and unrivalled panoramic view, also perfectly healthy. You will understand from this that what with having bought my team, tools, &c., it does not leave much for stock. One cow costs fifty dollars, and *hard* to get at that. A yearling calf costs from £3 to £5, and if possible I must try and get some in the fall, as I have put about seven acres into oats for hay, besides what hay I can cut (this having been a splendid season for grass). Oats would hardly pay to thresh on so small an acreage, though the yield ought to be between fifty and seventy bushels to the acre. Crops are magnificent. On lots of ranches *wheat* will go as high as fifty bushels to the acre this year (seventy-five have been raised). As my team, though strong, are not very heavy, I have only averaged three-quarters of an acre breaking sod a day. Three horses are generally used.

"With five cows I could keep twenty hogs, and what with my crop next year, garden, and work at odd times, should be considered rich here, and could put by money.

"You will perhaps remember my telling you that there was a saw-mill up the cañon above my ranche some three miles. Well, the 'boss' came down three weeks ago, and hired me to work for him at thirty dollars a month until threshing time, or the 1st of September. This suited me well, as on Sundays and after work, when not too tired, I could run down home and see that things were all right. B. is still staying with me, and is a great help. . . I started to work two days after, and stayed three weeks, whereas I had hoped to get a job till September. He shut down the mill suddenly, and thus threw me out of work. We have given him a piece of our mind, but as he was young, and didn't know his own mind, we didn't quarrel about it. This job, of course, suited me well, as it was handy to home ; but the day after to-morrow I am going after a three months' job on a sheep drive some three hundred miles, at forty dollars a month The sheep are twenty miles from here, and have to be driven down beyond Custer, which would bring me back home by threshing time.

"I am glad to say that wherever I have worked or am known at all I can always get a job, as I am considered to be a 'rustler,' or night-hawk, as I work early up to dark. The mill-owner is going to move his mill down to mouth of the cañon, I hear ; so this will to some extent improve the value of my property."

In July, 1885, he wrote to a friend :—

"I have only just received your letter. It has been a long time on the road, as I am now twenty miles away from home, working out at 'dipping sheep,' dirty and terribly hard work. As to your cousin coming out, I can only say that *I* certainly can do well, and I should say that he could also if he will be content to rough it. I have done nothing but rough it since I have been out, and find it has done me no harm, but much good. I am getting as strong as a horse.

"Thirty shillings (say five dollars) a week will keep your cousin in good circumstances; and if he cares to come out to me I can show him round, and he will be quite welcome. The climate is bracing, and it is without exception the healthiest place I have ever struck.

"Try and get 'the Old Man' [meaning *me*] to come out with you; you will enjoy the trip. I am sending this scrawl by a cowboy, and he may or may not forget to post it, though I trust he will not."

LETTER No. VI.

My last letter before leaving for the United States by the good ship "Cunardia."

London, August 20, 1885.

FRANK is now about twenty-six years of age. He has had four years of hard and varied experience, and although fortune has not yet smiled upon him, he does not seem inclined, so far as I am able to form an opinion from his correspondence, to succumb. I gather from his letters, by which alone I can at present judge, that he is still prepared to rough it. He has youth, health, and strength on his side, and I imagine there are few young fellows who have been brought up amidst the comforts and pleasures of a city life who would willingly have gone through so many handships.

Circumstances make it desirable for me to visit New York and the other Eastern cities. I have, therefore, resolved to journey so far as the Rockies, in order to see for myself, and thus to form a clear opinion of what he is doing and what his chances of success really are.

I propose, therefore, to follow up the foregoing sketch of Frank's four years' struggles by sending occasional letters, giving you an account of whatever may turn up on my long journey, and to describe what I may see of his location and surroundings. I am also not without hope of finding opportunities for some further piscatorial exploits in the lakes and streams of Montana. If I meet with any adventures in this way, I shall not fail to record them.

END OF PART I.

PART II.

LETTER No. VII.

On board the "Cunardia"—Small troubles—The Romance of a rickety old chair—Arrival at New York—First acquaintance with katydids.

New York, Sept., 1885.

IN travelling by land," says Washington Irving, "there is a continuity of scene and a connected succession of persons and incidents that lessen the effect of absence and separation. . . . But a wide sea-voyage severs us at once. It makes us conscious of being cast loose from the secure anchorage of settled life, and sent adrift upon a doubtful world. It interposes a gulf not merely imaginary, but real, between us and our homes—a gulf subject to tempest and fear and uncertainty, rendering distance palpable, and return precarious!"

That is just what I felt and thought, but could not find words to express so eloquently, "as I saw the last blue line of my native land fade away like a cloud in the horizon." Notwithstanding the fact that the broad Atlantic is now bridged over by seven-days' steamers, and linked to its Eastern and Western shores by submarine cables, as it was not in the Knickerbocker days, the solution of continuity seemed to me as real when I saw the last bit of rock as ever it was in that bygone time.

If I were writing a book of travels I should perhaps be tempted to tell you of all our little adventures in crossing the Atlantic. We had many small troubles which at the time we thought large ones; but why should I record such every-day occurrences? There was a time when we would have given "a thousand furlongs of sea for an acre of barren ground—long heath, brown furze, anything." We had quite enough of the rough to remind even the best of us that, when rolled and tossed in "the roaring forties," "we're all poor creeters"—and again, we had enough of the delightfully smooth to satisfy us that perhaps we are not such "poor creeters" after all. We reached New York only ten hours after the usual time.

One little story may be worth telling. On the fifth day out, when the westerly gale had partly subsided, but while the weather was still muggy and cold, I had been sitting on a rickety chair next to what seemed to be a bundle of rugs. When I got up, a gust of wind tilted the chair rather roughly against the bundle, and I then observed that it began to move. I immediately turned to apologize to this living and moving bundle. A pair of bright blue eyes peeped out, and a pleasant voice explained to me that my unmannerly chair had been no inconvenience at all. The bright eyes and pleasant voice were, as I soon found, the property of a charming young lady, with whom I had a long chat, and we soon became very good friends. Stress of weather had kept her a prisoner below, and this was her first appearance in the upper regions. I, as you know,

am only an old "buffer," but my friend
and travelling companion M. is a bright
young spark, with a heart like a tinder-box,
and when he came round and I had introduced
him, he was at once smitten with the
charms which had gradually unfolded themselves
from the rugs. Soon afterwards
my friend M. introduced (though I think
with somewhat jealous misgivings) another
young acquaintance; and this fine fellow
at once fell a victim to the fascinations
which had already fluttered M.'s susceptible
heart.

It was amusing enough to such an old
fellow as I to watch the antics of these
young people. We supped together, and we
paraded the deck. When we reached New
York, our hotels being within a stone's throw
of each other, we frequently met.

M., whose chivalry at least equalled his
infatuation, suppressed his own ardour in
favour of his friend's. They went to the
theatre together, they supped at Delmonico's,
and in two days the young and happy couple
were engaged to be married. I don't think
I shall betray any special confidence when I

add that the young lady was on her way with her brother to her native home at the Antipodes, and that the successful smitten one was a wealthy *ranchero* of the Far West. When the happy secret was confided to me I gave them my paternal blessing and we all separated—he hastening off to his hunting grounds to sell his immense stock of cattle and sheep, and then to meet his young *fiancée* and her brother at San Francisco, thence to proceed together to Australia to settle affairs with "papa."

This little episode, probably not an uncommon one on board ship, though quite new to me, I will call "*The Romance of a Rickety Old Chair.*"

The heat was so oppressive when we arrived at New York, that we were well pleased to accept the kind invitation of a friend to spend a night at his pleasant residence on the Sound.

Here it was that I first heard, and was gradually lulled to sleep by the incessant singing of little green katydids in the surrounding trees. What a curious monody their combined song makes! It varies the note, as it seemed to me, to something like this :—

>Katy-did, Katy-did, Katy-didn't,
>Katy-*did*, Katy-didn't, Katy-*did*,
>Katy-*didn't*, Katy-did, Katy-didn't.

Such was the unchanging song of myriads of these little creatures for hours at a time; and to this was added the chirping of grasshoppers and locusts, and a perpetual accompaniment of the shrill little shriek of tree-toads.

The lovely autumn evening, a pleasant sail on the Sound, the green foliage of the trees, and these little insect-songs were refreshing to me after our rough and rolling experiences on the Atlantic.

LETTER No. VIII.

Up the Hudson River—The Catskills—My first chipmunk—"The Rip Van Winkle"—"Sleepy Hollow"—The Mountain-House Hotel—Old Indian squaw-spirit—A snake in the grass—A painting by Holbein.

Catskill Mountains, Sept., 1885.

AFTER a short time in New York, agreeably spent in spite of the heat, we started early one bright morning on the splendid river steamer "Albany" up the noble Hudson River. It is no part of my plan or my duty to describe the innumerable objects, historical and picturesque, which command this wonderful river. Why should I attempt to describe or even to mention points so fully and so well described elsewhere? All I aspire to record is the passing impression of whatever comes under my own notice or interests me as a rapid traveller; it would be presumption to do more.

The chief object and *ultima Thule* of my wanderings is that little log shanty built by my boy thousands of miles away in the heart of the Rocky Mountains—but our plan is to take in our way as much of this great country as our limited time will permit.

The point we are now sailing for is "The Catskills," about 120 miles up the river from New York. Reaching the Catskill Station early in the afternoon, we took train for the foot of the mountains, a ride of about eight miles through a richly cultivated country: every object here, even the rocks and streams and fruit-laden apple-trees, seemed strange and new to me.

At the foot of the ascent, we were met by a stage-wagon drawn by a couple of stout horses; these had to drag us for three miles and a half up the steep mountain side.

The mountain is clad with thick foliage to the summit. The sun was shining hotly, but we were protected by a canopy formed of the green leaves of trees mostly new to me.

Scattered freely among them were maples decked in manifold autumn tints, several kinds of birch, and oaks with leaves differing so much in shape from any English oaks I know, that I should not have called these young saplings oaks at all but for the unmistakable large acorns with which they were laden. Then, too, there were the mountain-ash with large chocolate cones, and the lovely sumach with red berries. The mingling of this variegated foliage made for me an indescribably pleasant scene.

What has much surprised and pleased me in this, the first American wood I have seen, is the fresh, bright, spring-like greenness of the leaves, at a time when in Old England leaves are becoming sere and brown, and are rapidly falling.

We had no sooner entered the wood than I saw sitting on a rail a pretty little animal of a kind unknown to me. It was the size of a small squirrel, but without the bushy upturned tail. I had but a glimpse as it darted away; it was brown on the back, with broad black diagonal stripes, and white throat and belly. The driver told me it was a chipmunk—it may have had three inches of tail.

The road for some distance up was alive with katydids and locusts; but birds and other animals seem to be very scarce. I was told there are plenty of jack-rabbits and part-

"THE RIP VAN WINKLE."

ridges in these woods, and occasionally a black bear is heard of.

Apart from the music of the katydids and grasshoppers there is perfect stillness; and one longs to hear the songs of birds in these pleasant places, but I never heard even "the occasional whistle of a quail or tapping of a woodpecker."

Halfway up the hill we came upon an old-fashioned little inn called "The Rip Van Winkle," and the stone on which Rip slept. His long sleep is regarded as a true and veritable piece of history about which there can be no question, for is not the rock still there to attest it?

Over the porch is a half-obliterated signboard representing Rip Van Winkle waking up, and underneath is the inscription,—

"O that flagon! that wicked flagon! what shall I say to Dame Winkle?"[1]

Here it was that "from an opening between the trees" Rip "could overlook all the lower country for many a mile of rich woodland. He saw at a distance the lordly Hudson, far, far below him, moving on in its silent but majestic course." Here it is that we look down through the foliage upon " Sleepy Hollow," at least I was told so by the communicative landlord; certainly the opening does reveal a deep wood-clad valley, which looks charming, though somnolent enough to merit

[1] It should read "What excuse shall I make to Dame Van Winkle?"

the title of "Sleepy Hollow;" nevertheless, Knickerbocker's "Sleepy Hollow" is certainly not here; it lies away down yonder "in the bosom of one of those spacious coves which indent the eastern shore of the Hudson, not far from the village of Tarrytown, in a little valley or rather lap of land among high hills, which is one of the quietest places in the whole world."

Some of us walked up the steep inclines to ease the horses, until we reached "The Mountain-House Hotel," a great place capable of holding five hundred people; but the season is over, and there are not more than thirty here now; the other hotels on the mountains are already closed. I will only say of this hostelry that it is kept in a very primitive style, and is certainly fifty years behind the age.

The view from the front, on the very edge of the cliff, looks over a semicircle of country extending for sixty miles in every direction, with the Hudson River winding like a silver streak through the very heart of it. This prospect, they tell me, is one of the most wonderful to be found in this wonderful country, but owing to haze and mist it is rarely to be seen as we saw it.

We wandered through the woods and down by the lakes for miles, but we heard not a sound of bird or beast; the dead silence is almost appalling; not even the noisy little katydids get so far up the mountains.

These woods would be perfect if one could only say of them as Longfellow says of some of the American woods in autumn :

"The gentle wind, a sweet and passionate wooer,
Kisses the blushing leaf, and stirs up life
Within the solemn woods of ash deep-crimsoned,
And silver beech, and maple yellow-leaved,
Where Autumn, like a faint old man, sits down
By the wayside aweary. Through the trees
The golden robin moves. The purple finch,
That on wild cherry and red cedar feeds,
A winter bird, comes with its plaintive whistle,
And pecks by the witch-hazel, whilst aloud
From cottage roofs the warbling bluebird sings."

The weather during our stay here has been perfect, the air bright and bracing; that old Indian squaw-spirit who is said to influence the weather on the "Catskills," "spreading sunshine or clouds over the landscape," was very good to us; she gave us nothing but bright sunshiny days and clear moonlight nights, a sure proof that we were welcome visitors, for it is said that when she is displeased she " would brew up clouds black as ink, sitting in the midst of them like a bottle-bellied spider in the midst of its web; and when these clouds broke, woe betide the valleys!"

We visited most of the points of interest within easy reach. There is a magnificent waterfall near the Laurel House, and many other sights which it did us good to see. The sunset one night was the most glorious I had ever beheld. " Real handsome," a Baltimorean enthusiast called it, and the full silver moon shining over the broad expanse was equally " handsome."

One morning, as I was walking along the cliff in front of the hotel, a snake nearly a yard long sprang out of the long grass under my feet, and flung itself right over the precipice; it came down flop on the hard rock thirty feet below, and then shot off into the bushes as if there was nothing the matter. The whole thing passed so rapidly that I could not distinctly note the colour of the reptile; but it seemed to be of a dark-brownish colour. I wondered if that was its usual way of going home, or if it had made the leap by mistake.

A SNAKE FLUNG ITSELF OVER THE PRECIPICE.

That snake, the little chipmunk, katydids, and sparrows, were the only samples I saw of the natural history of "The Catskills;" but it must be remembered that I only passed two days there. Even the idle Rip, however, could find but little sport for his vagabond gun, for he is said to have "trudged through woods and swamps, and up hill and down dale, to shoot a few squirrels or wild pigeons."

I was told by the landlord, who, proud of the grand position he holds as monarch of a sixty-miles' unrivalled panorama, must have told it scores of times before, that down yonder in the village of Catskill there resides a member of the Salisbury family, who possesses a family picture painted by Holbein which he regards as of priceless value. This good and loquacious old landlord is full of the history of the great valley and river in front of him, and if you have patience to listen he will tell you everything that ever happened from the time when Hendrich Hudson first discovered it to the present time.

LETTER No. IX.

Arrival at Saratoga—Season over—Hotel crowded with Deputies for nomination of a State Governor—Mugwump—Arrival at Niagara—The Falls at midnight and by moonlight—No letter from Frank.

Niagara Falls, Sept., 1885.

E left the "Catskills" on a Monday morning for Saratoga; but the glory of Saratoga had departed; the season was all but over; only a few stragglers of the flock of the summer birds of fashion remained, the others had already migrated southward. The shopkeepers were packing up their goods and shutting up their shops, and resident hibernators were preparing their winter quarters; but the great hotel was not empty. On the

contrary, we found it difficult to procure a night's lodging there. The house was crowded, but not with youth and beauty; there was no sound of music and of revelry, but there was a great clatter of the tongues of men—strong, healthy, earnest-looking men, who had come from every village in New York State to "vote their ticket." It was the time of convention for nomination of a Governor for the State.

It was pleasant to me to be afforded an opportunity of seeing such an assemblage of true American men in one hall. I presume that every man I saw in that great crowd was the chosen representative of his own village or parish or township or city; and I own I was agreeably surprised to observe that so very many of them bore such a strong family resemblance to the best of my own countrymen of the like class; the chief difference perhaps being one which I regard as favourable to the Americans, for they did not smoke so much as so many Englishmen would have done, and certainly they drank far less. Indeed, I noticed that many of them confined their drinks to iced water, or tea and coffee. There was very little spitting, and I am pretty sure there was no chewing. Their cheeks were bronzed and healthy, and they had the appearance of intelligent men, quite in earnest respecting the the business they had come to do.

I fancy that the men assembled in this hotel were all bent on voting the Republican ticket, while the Democrats had met in other quarters. Here it was that for the first time I learnt the existence of a third party in the State which rejoices in the title of " Mugwump."

I have not been able to find this word in any American dictionary, but it seems to have become so thoroughly imbedded in the American language that you may be quite sure it will be found with its derivation and application fully described and probably illustrated in that grand new dictionary now being prepared by "The Century Company." My present information, however, only enables me to say that a "mugwump" is a man who has earned that appellation on account of his strict adherence to the dictates of his own conscience; he votes for principle, not for party. A "mugwump" is a man who, if he is a Republican, will vote for a good Democrat rather than for a bad Republican, and probably the converse holds good. Of course I repelled the idea that honesty was so rare amongst American politicians as to have led them to invent a new word to represent such an unusual phenomenon as an honest voter; there is, I am sure, a better reason to be found, and I commend the word to the notice of English politicians; the principle it represents may be valuab'e if largely applied during our own coming elections.

We took a rapid survey, by a drive round the park and the lake, and then went "aboard" the cars for Niagara.

The Falls of Niagara.

We had a long cold ride through the night, and our hotel being on the Canadian side, we caught our first sight of the Falls under unusual circumstances; in fact, through the windows of a large omnibus occupied by ourselves alone, and driven slowly over the Suspension Bridge at two o'clock in the morning. The harvest moon, just at its full, but a little

THE FALLS, FROM THE SUSPENSION BRIDGE.

obscured by passing clouds and mists, was shining on the Falls, and, as the horses tramped slowly over the bridge, suspended several hundred feet above the dread waters, we came upon the scene quite unexpectedly : the sight was a stirring one, I assure you. On the bridge we could see the whole of the Falls at once, looking down upon them from our great height.

The Falls looked at in this way, from a moving carriage suspended in the air, were somewhat dwarfed in height ; of course we could get but a glimpse in passing in the night. We expected to have been stunned by the roar of the Falls, but our first surprise was at the awful silence ; we could hear nothing but the tramp of the horses and the roll of the wheels as our carriage moved slowly along—all else was silent as the grave. Notwithstanding the moonlight, it was not clear enough to distinguish motion in the Falls above us or in the water far down beneath us. The great semicircular Horseshoe, as we passed along in front of it, looked as though a great white sheet had been thrown over its motionless face, and the foam and stir of the water below was fixed and immovable as in a painted picture.

No motion was to be discerned anywhere, the moonlight was too hazy. I assure you that was a weird and grand picture we saw last night; the Falls beheld dimly, indistinctly, and really through a glass darkly—and so we arrived at the Clifton House Hotel.

The next day arose, like every other we have yet seen on this American Continent, bright and beautiful. We had only one day to see everything, so we took a drive round.

I am not going to attempt a description or to rhapsodize over the Falls of Niagara—great authors have done so over and over again. Charles Dickens has moralized about them; Anthony Trollope has described them; William Black has painted their portraits in bright words—why should I attempt to describe them? To me these great waters seem to say, " Men may come and stare at us, and men may go, but we flow on irresistibly and for ever. We care nought for your staring, your admiration, your poetic fancies about us. We are matter-of-fact; stare as much as you please, but come not within our grip.

Build your airy roads above us, span us over if you will, but know that death and destruction await him who dares to come within the proscribed limit of our rapids above or our whirlpools below. You may sail on our placid waters up yonder, your ' Maid of the Mist ' may approach the outer circle of our Falls below, but come not within that circle, or we shall have you in a grip from which no power on earth shall save you." The scene, the picture, is indelibly impressed on my memory, and there it must remain. I will not spoil that picture by daring to paint it in feeble words.

We did what is usual in our limited time. We drove down to the Whirlpool, we crossed the suspension bridge, we wandered through Goat Island, we descended beneath the Horseshoe Falls to the utmost point allowed by the guide. We had our portraits taken in the subaquatic costume, but so hideously did they come out that we promptly suppressed them.

The people who live at the Falls are quite aware of it. Every individual regards them as his own property; even in the coldest

IN THE ROCKIES.

weather dollars melt there like snow in summer's heat; so we were glad to get away from Niagara and its army of vampires.

Here at Niagara I fully expected letters from Frank. I have now been fourteen days in America, and he knows it, and yet not a line of welcome to these shores has he sent me. To-morrow we turn our faces to the West; surely at Chicago, which is 536 miles from hence, I shall get some news of him.

LETTER No. X.

Start for Chicago—"The Michigan Central"—Arrival at Chicago—Still no letter from Frank—Start for St. Paul—St. Paul and Minneapolis—Commodore Kitson's stables—Falls of St. Anthony—"The Granary of the World"—Falls of Minnehaha—Telegram to Frank.

St. Paul, Minnesota, Oct., 1885.

N the morning of our start for the West we were aroused before five o'clock to catch a train which did not reach our station till 8.30.

The line over which we travelled to Chicago was "The Michigan Central," which runs along the north side of Lake Erie to Windsor; at this point the train is carried bodily across the Detroit river to Detroit on an enormous barge built for the purpose; from thence we proceed to Chicago. Nothing befell us by the way, and I have only to remark about the railway that the carriages were very comfortable, or rather would have been so but for the stifling extent to which they were heated. The dining-car is well managed, and the food excellent. We reached Chicago at ten o'clock the same night, after a long, dusty, and very hot journey, through not particularly interesting scenery.

We have now got a thousand miles on our way to look after the young *ranchero*, but where is he? Why does he not write? I was growing anxious, for up to this time I had not received a line, and no letter awaited me here. I telegraphed to him, but no reply came. I wrote requesting that a telegram might meet me at St. Paul, over four hundred miles farther on our route.

We were most hospitably entertained by our friends, and after hurriedly driving round the points of interest in Chicago, we made another departure, still for the Far West. Here we take the Chicago and North Western Railroad for St. Paul. This iron road claims to be "the best and most perfectly equipped railway in the world;" its luxuriantly furnished drawing-room coaches are marvels of beauty and comfort, and the dining-cars are superb; the meals and attendance are equal to what one might expect to find in any first-class hotel, and I can bear most willing testimony to the civility we met with from all the officials, from the chief passenger manager down to the road attendants.

We left Chicago at 9.55 p.m., and we reached St. Paul at 2.25 p.m. next day, a distance of 409 miles.

As regards time, I may mention that American railway companies deal very arbitrarily with the sun.[1] At Niagara he is bidden to stand still in the heavens for one hour, and is called Eastern time. Then he makes a sudden jump to Mandan, 476 miles west of St. Paul; over this space, viz., one hour, he is called Central time; then from Mandan to Heron (1,429 miles west of St. Paul), he makes another leap and is called Mountain time. From Heron to Portland on the Pacific he again recedes an hour, and is

[1] See Appendix (page 214) for Time Diagram.

called Pacific time. This hop, skip, and jump across the American continent, in lieu of his usual steady mode of progression, is of course a very convenient arrangement for railways, and it appears to be universally accepted. I suppose he makes the same hourly jumps on the same longitudinal lines throughout the continent. It will thus be seen that the sun rises and sets four hours later at Portland than at New York.

St. Paul, the capital of Minnesota, is a very flourishing and beautiful city built on a series of terraces on the left or eastern bank of the great " Father of Waters," over which it commands magnificent views. The streets are paved with pine-logs, over which one travels in comfort that contrasts most favourably with the rough and clumsy paving-stones of New York. Minneapolis is situated ten miles further west, on the right bank of the Mississippi. In 1860 the combined population of the two cities was 16,000—to-day it exceeds 250,000. They are rapidly approaching each other, and the time is looked forward to when they will form one great metropolitan city. Within the last three

years they have doubled their population.
They are now called "The Twin Cities,"
though their commercial interests are not
identical, and there is considerable rivalry
between the two cities.

We were driven out by a friend of M.'s,

ST. PAUL.

whom we met at the hotel, to a place called
Midway Park, where Commodore Kitson
keeps his celebrated trotters. Here we were
shown the fastest trotters and pacers in the
world. "Johnston," the "King of the Turf,"
was trotted out for our inspection. I am no

judge of horseflesh, though I tried to look as knowing as I possibly could. We were told that in *pacing*—which I think means trotting by advancing the two right legs together and then the two left legs, like the celebrated animal in Miss Thompson's " Roll Call "—he is the fastest horse in the world; to me, who am uninitiated, his trot looked like an awkward shamble; but he paces a mile in 2 min. $6\frac{1}{4}$ sec. Our attention was drawn to the large bumps on his forehead—a proof, his trainer said, of very unusual intellect. We were also shown " Little Brown Jug," " Fanny Witherspoon," and " Minnie R.," all well-known names in the sporting world. " Minnie R. " it appears paced a mile in 2 min. $3\frac{1}{4}$ sec. with "Firebrand" trotting alongside; this I presume is a great help.

These stables are admirably arranged. Each animal lives in a sort of little drawing-room, decorated with flags, pictures, and records of deeds accomplished. I much regretted my extreme ignorance with respect to these worldwide wonders, but I was careful not to betray it. There were many other horses pointed out to us, but I forget their names.

I was told they were not to be matched in the wide world, and not one of them was worth less than 20,000 dollars — probably there was a little vain boasting in this. The same day I cut the following from a St. Paul paper :—

> "The death of George Wilkes, the editor (of 'The Spirit of the Times'), and 'Goldsmith Maid,' the trotter, on the same day, may not be a very singular thing, after all, but a St. Paul horseman remarked yesterday that it was 'a queer coincidence that two such old and well-known sports should fly the track on the home stretch together.'"

I rather think the "Goldsmith Maid" had been a thorn in the side of the sanguine headboss of the Kitson stables. I knew poor Wilkes well many years ago, not however in his capacity as sportsman, but as author of a work on Shakespeare, the main object of which, if my memory serves me, was to prove that the Swan of Avon was a "bloated aristocrat!"

We had not time to stay at Minneapolis, and could only catch a slight glimpse of its magnificent bridges and corn elevators as our train swept by.

Here, somewhere in the immediate neighbourhood of Minneapolis, are the celebrated Falls of St. Anthony, and also those of Minnehaha, which we would gladly have gone to see had time permitted. We were told, however, that their charms are not less practical than poetic.

The practical charms of Minneapolis, St. Anthony's Falls, and the surrounding country, are demonstrated in the following cutting from "Forest and Stream":—

"THE GRANARY OF THE WORLD.

"So it has been called, this northern land of lakes and forests and broad prairies. And the appellation is not altogether fanciful. Visit Minneapolis and inspect its flouring mills, inquire as to their number and the capacity of each, and you will find that the annual product of flour from this source is enough to supply the world with bread—for a while at least. These mills can turn out thirty thousand barrels of flour per day, when running on full time, and at this rate their product for a year would supply one-quarter of the population of the United States with the bread which they annually consume. It may be taken for granted that these mills have not been established here without some good reason. The great water-power of the Falls of St. Anthony is usually alleged as the cause of the growth of this tremendous industry, but that alone would not be enough to have brought it into existence and to have raised it to its present proportions. The true cause is that the whole vast country from the Mississippi to the Rocky Mountains, all through Minnesota, Dakota, and Montana, is a wheat-producing country, all of the product of which is tributary to the city where these mills are located."

And was it not at the wonderful " Falls of Minnehaha" near by—

> "That my Hiawatha halted
> In the land of the Dacotahs?
>   Was it not to see the maiden,
> See the face of Laughing Water
> Peeping from behind the curtain;
> Hear the rustling of her garments
> From behind the waving curtain,
> As one sees the Minnehaha
> Gleaming, glancing through the branches—
> As one hears the Laughing Water
> From behind its screen of branches?"

We had now to travel by the Northern Pacific Railroad for 1,200 miles. Before beginning this long journey I was anxious to hear something of Frank, for no telegram or letter had even yet reached me. I am indebted to the general passenger manager at St. Paul, Mr. Chas. S. Fee, for his great courtesy in sending the following telegram, free of cost to me, to his own agent at Bozeman:—

FALLS OF MINNEHAHA.

"Mr. ——, of London, desires that his son, Frank M., whose post-office is Bozeman, shall meet him in Livingston next Wednesday, on arrival of number one. He desires that he shall come equipped for a five days' trip in the Park. Drop this telegram in the post-office at once.—C. S. F."

Livingston is the station about twenty-five miles east of Bozeman, where we branch off southward for the Yellowstone National Park; and I thought surely this would stir the boy up, if alive and well. I need hardly say that my anxiety was increasing. My feverish desire now is to get on to Livingston, as quickly as possible, and my next letter will, I hope, be dated from Frank's abode.

LETTER No. XI.

The North Pacific Railway—Brainerd—Detroit—
Massacre by Sioux—Indian Reservation—Fargo—
Wheat-fields of Dakota—Bismarck—"Bad Lands"
—The Rockies—Arrival at Livingston.

Frank's Ranche, Oct., 1885.

WE took our departure from St. Paul in a Pullman Sleeping Car at 4 p.m., and found ourselves very comfortably placed; a fortunate circumstance, seeing that this car had to be our home for fifty-eight hours over 1,032 miles from St. Paul to Livingston, with no opportunity of even stretching our legs outside the train.

The North Pacific Railroad stretches across the great continent from Duluth at the head of Lake Superior, and from St. Paul, the capital of Minnesota, to Portland, on the Pacific, a distance of nearly 2,000 miles.

Of its commercial success or the value of its shares in the market I know nothing, but as a simple traveller over more than 1,200

DINING CAR.

miles I can speak well of it; its track is all steel rail, and its road-bed solid. All its passenger trains are equipped with the Westinghouse air-brake, Miller platforms, and patent steel-tired car-wheels. Pullman palace drawing-room sleeping-cars of the newest and most improved pattern run between St. Paul and Portland; I would, however, caution passengers that it is desirable to secure berths in these beforehand at St. Paul, by applying to the conductor, who will telegraph to the ticket agents in advance. The dining-cars are also very luxurious in their appointments, and the *menu* all that can be desired. I may add that the charge for every meal is only seventy-five cents, whereas I have been charged a dollar on other lines, and at inconvenient roadside inns, for far inferior fare. The only complaint I have to make is that the cars are sometimes heated in a way which is almost unbearable, and if they could increase their speed, which averages seventeen miles an hour, it would be a boon to weary travellers who want to get on. One does not object to moderate progress through beautiful scenery, but seventeen miles an hour for hundreds of miles of prairie land becomes monotonous.

From St. Paul our route takes a north-westerly direction on the eastern side of the

Mississippi to Brainerd, where the railroad from Duluth joins our line. There we cross the Mississippi, and thenceforth our route is almost in a bee-line due west to the Pacific. On leaving Brainerd we pass through the Lake Park region, and for some distance the scenery is charmingly diversified by fine timber and lakes, on which may be seen flocks of wild ducks and larger water-fowl, sometimes a solitary prairie chicken, and here and there a well-fenced wheat farm with good buildings, and surrounded by many large ricks. In the neighbourhood of Detroit, Min., is the White Earth Reservation of the Chippewa or Ojibway Indians, of whom there are 1,500 civilized and Christianized. It is only about twenty years ago that this country was devastated by the murderous Sioux, when more than 3,000 men, women, and children were most inhumanly butchered.

Now we reach Fargo, and are in the neighbourhood of the famous wheat-fields of Dakota.

"It is in this neighbourhood that those enormous farms are located which extend further than the eye

MR. G. DALKAMILL'S FARM.

can reach, and upon which in harvest time an army of labourers are employed. One of the largest of these belongs to a firm of which Mr. Oliver Dalrymple is the chief. They own about 75,000 acres, or 117 square miles.—*Forest and Stream.*

At Bismarck we crossed the Missouri river ("the big muddy," as it is called), over a splendid three-pier iron bridge. The view one gets of the upward reach of the river and its muddy banks is fine. The bridge has three spans of 400 feet each and two approach spans of 113 feet each; it is said to have cost a million dollars. The Missouri is here 3,500 miles from the Gulf of Mexico, and 2,800 feet wide, being still navigable for 2,000 miles further to the north.

At Mandan we come upon Mountain time, that is, we lose an hour since leaving Niagara. We reached Mandan at 12.50, and started at 12.10 by the time-table, having remained there twenty minutes. We are now approaching Pyramid Park, the celebrated " Bad Lands," but our train is two hours behind time, so we shall not see them by daylight, and in fact I failed to see them at all.

When I arose on the following morning at

BRIDGE ACROSS THE MISSOURI AT BISMARCK.

six o'clock we found ourselves travelling along

> "That desolate land and lone,
> Where the Big Horn and Yellowstone
> Roar down their mountain path."

We had passed Bad Lands in the night. I cannot pretend to describe what I did not see, but I am told that this extraordinary bit of country is in itself worth coming from England to see; there is nothing else in the world like it. One writer tells me that "it owes its singular appearance to the combined action of fuel and water, which have assisted to produce the most fantastic forms and startling contrasts of colours that the most disordered imagination could conceive."

Mr. E. V. Smalley thus describes it:—

"The change in the scene is so startling, and the appearance of the landscape so wholly novel and so singularly grotesque, that you rub your eyes to make sure that you are not dreaming of some ancient geologic epoch, when the rude, unfinished earth was the sport of Titanic forces, or fancying yourself transported to another planet. Enormous masses of conglomerate—red, grey, black, brown, and blue, in towers, pyramids, peaks, ridges, domes, castellated heights—occupy the face of the country. In the spaces

IN THE ROCKIES.

between are grassy, lawn-like expanses, dotted with the petrified stumps of huge trees. The finest effect of colour is produced by the dark red rock—not rock in fact, but actual terra-cotta, baked by the heat of underlying layers of lignite. At some points the coal

"BAD LANDS."

is still on fire, and the process of transforming mountains of blue clay into mountains of pottery may be observed from day to day. It has been going on for countless ages, no doubt. To bake one of these colossal masses may have required 10,000 years of smouldering heat. I despair of giving any adequate idea of the fantastic forms of the buttes or of the wonderful effects of colour they offer. The pen and brush of a skilful artist would alone be competent for the task. The photographer, be he never so deft with his camera and chemicals, only belittles these marvellous views. He catches only bare outlines, without colour, and colour is the chief thing in the picture. He cannot get the true effect of distance, and his negatives show only staring blacks and whites in place of the infinite variations of light and shadow effects in valleys and gorges and hollows, and upon crags and pinnacles. Look, if you can, by the feeble aid of written words, upon a single butte, and see how impossible it is to photograph it satisfactorily. It rises from a carpet of green grass. Its base has a bluish hue, and appears to be clay solidified by enormous pressure. It is girdled by bands of light grey stone and black lignite coal. Its upper portion is of the rich red colour of old Egyptian pottery. Crumbled fragments strew its sides. Its summit, rising 300 feet above the plain, has been carved by the elements into turrets, battlements, sharp spires, grotesque gargoyles, and huge projecting buttresses—an amazing jumble of weird architectural effects, that startle the eye with suggestions of intelligent design. Above, the sky is wonderfully clear and blue, the rays of the setting sun spread a rosy tint over the crest, and just above its highest tower floats a little flame-coloured cloud like a banner. When I say there are thousands of these buttes, the reader will perceive that the Bad Lands of the Little Missouri are a region of extraordinary interest to the tourist and artist."

I had done my best to keep awake; I really thought I had done so for hours, and I know that I peeped out of my bed many times during the night, but nothing but the dim broad everlasting prairie met my gaze—so I must have fallen asleep just as we were passing through this interesting region, to my great disappointment. I was told by those who had been more wakeful, that they could see the lignite coal a-fire,—fire which has for countless ages been baking these rocks into actual terra-cotta. I was inclined to question the exactness of this statement. Smoke may doubtless be seen; and when I am told by a man that he has lighted a cigar at a hole in the rock the existence of fire can be no longer questioned.

We were told by the guide-books to expect to see hereabouts, herds of buffalo, deer, and elk,—in fact, we have only seen a few prairie dogs, and these looked comical enough as they stood bolt upright on their little hillocks, with their fore-paws hanging down before them. They only wanted a stick in their arms to look like soldiers on guard.

Just here we caught our first distant glimpse of the Rockies, some of the peaks tipped with snow,—and now we are at Livingston!

I need not tell you how anxiously I looked out for the train from Bozeman. When it came in I sought in vain through the crowd for Frank; my heart sank within me when I found that no Frank was there. I could not get on to Bozeman; the last train for the day had already gone, so we took the train for the "National Park," and I sat down in one corner of it, and felt more like fainting than I had ever felt in my life before. Three weeks had I been in the country, and not a word or sign from the boy I had come so far to see. What was the cause? If he had been ill some friend would surely have told me. Was he living? Had he met with some terrible accident on that long sheep-drive he wrote about months ago? Had he married a red Indian squaw, and did he not want to see me? Did he suppose that his old friend M. and I would be too proud to put up at the little log shanty which he had built with his own hands? Had he been in the hug of a grizzly?

These were some of the grim reflections that passed through my disturbed mind as I sat at the end of the car, gloomily watching the magnificent scenery through which the train was now carrying us down towards the Park.

LETTER No. XII.

The Yellowstone National Park—"The New Wonderland"—"The Devil's Slide"—The stage driver—Story of a corpse—Driving a circus coach—Circus Bill "appropriates" a coat—Stealing their own blankets—Start for the Park—Mammoth Springs—Forest of dead pines—The Lake of the Woods—Norris Hot Springs and Geysers—"Hell's Half-acre"—A perilous drive—Fire Hole River - Lower Geyser Springs—"Old Faithful"—"The Bee Hive"—The Grand Cañon—Rough roads—Return—"The Golden Gate"—"By Jove! it's Frank!"

Frank's Ranche, Oct., 1885.

THE Yellowstone National Park lies partly in the territory of Wyoming and partly in that of Montana. It is sixty-five miles north and south, by fifty-five miles east and west; it comprises 3,575 square miles, and is throughout its extent 6,000 feet or more above the level of the sea. The mountain ranges that hem in the valleys on every side rise to a height of from 10,000 to 12,000 feet, and are covered with perpetual snow.

The Yellowstone Park is a perfect little world of wonders. They call it the "New Wonderland," and there are as many strange things to be found in it as "Alice" saw in her fairy realm.

On reaching Livingston, we take a train which runs southward to within six miles of the entrance to the Park. Soon after leaving the station we pass through a grand cañon of towering rocks called "The Gate of the Mountains," and then through pleasant valleys, always near the beautiful Yellowstone river.

We then pass, on our right, Cinnabar Mountain, which rises to a height of about 2,000 feet above the river; a broad streak of red down the mountain is called "The Devil's Slide," and suggests at the same time that his black majesty in sliding down must have had a rough time of it.

The terminus of the line is at a place called Cinnabar City, which at present contains about twelve shanties; several of these are drinking saloons. From Cinnabar we take a stage-coach and six horses for the drive, through some very grand scenery, to the "Mammoth

Springs Hotel." The driver of this stage is a fellow of infinite wit, and tells marvellous stories in a manner which kept us on a roar the whole way. I wish I could give you, in

"THE GATE OF THE MOUNTAINS."

his own style and words, the story of a corpse which he once carried on his coach.

"Once," said he, "I was driving a coach down in Utah—a sixty-mile drive. One night a corpse came along, packed in a leaden coffin, and then in a wooden one, and then in a box. They fixed him on the top of the stage. Of course we had no passengers; who would want to travel with a corpse if they could help it? It was a bitter cold and pitchy dark night, sometimes snowing and raining, with lightning and thunder. The way that blessed corpse kept rolling backwards and forwards on the top of the coach was, I tell you, pretty scaring. For about thirty miles the road ran along the side of a mountain. You bet I whipped them horses along, and my off-wheels travelled in the air most of the way. I got to the end of my journey two hours quicker than I ever done that journey before. I am not a bit superstitious; but driving a corpse all alone over the mountains on a night like that isn't very lively. If I had known the party in the box it might have been different, but we were strangers. Next time a corpse comes along wanting a ride with me, I guess he'll have to walk. I never want to drive another."

Charlie told us that he was once the driver of a circus coach—

"And I tell you," said he, "that was an experience! The pay wasn't much, a hundred dollars a month or so; the rest was made up by appropriation! I had a trunk full of things when I started, but I hadn't been driving a week before everything was gone out of it, and then they stole the trunk. I had nothing left but what I stood up in, and I asked a fellow-driver what I was to do. 'Do?' says he; 'why don't you take a coat?' The next hotel we stopped at, 'Circus Bill,' that was his name, stood round and unhooked a splendid buffalo coat. I wore that coat all winter, and then sold it in the spring to a Mormon in Salt Lake City for seventy-five dollars, which about repaid me for the loss of my own trunk. I once knew two of them fellows who got drunk and stole their own blankets, and were locked up for it!"

As we were going along he pointed out an eagle's nest on the top of a pinnacle of the

mountain. Presently we arrived at Gardener City, a flourishing place of a dozen dwellings. It was now getting towards sundown. "Won't you have a lantern, colonel, for the rest of the road?" "No, thanks," said our driver; "the brightness of my face and the brilliancy of my wit are quite sufficient to light up the road."

The Mammoth Hot Springs Hotel is large and commodious, and for a summer resort fairly comfortable ; it is capable of accommodating 400 guests. In the hall is a splendid specimen of a mountain lion, bearing in his mouth the significant inscription, " Meet me by moonlight alone !" The hotel faces the famous Mammoth Springs, of which the accompanying sketch gives but a very imperfect idea. The hill is about 200 feet high, composed of the chalky deposit of the hot springs, and the series of terraces present a marvellous scene ; but they do not, however, exhibit that beautiful clear snowy whiteness which some enthusiasts claim for them ; they have rather the appearance of dirty, crumbling, whitey-brown chalk.

Next morning we started off on a coach and four to view the Park. First we came to "The Golden Gates," an immense cañon through which a small stream runs between enormously high limestone rocks. The road, which is here a splendid one, winds up along one side of the cañon ; it is cut out of the solid rock, and it gradually rises to such a height that to a nervous person the look down into the gulch below must be rather alarming, especially if one had not the fullest confidence in the driver. Then we passed through an extraordinary forest of pines, all dead, stripped entirely of their bark, even to the gnarled and curled branches. There must be millions of these naked-burnt trees

"THE OBSIDIAN CLIFFS."

standing, and the ground is also strewed with them in every direction. Here and there the upturned roots present a very weird and curious appearance. One made a strong impression on me from its marked resemblance to that wonderful griffin which now commemorates the spot where once stood Temple Bar.

We crossed the Gardener river, then passed

below an extraordinary range called "The Obsidian Cliffs." They are composed of glass—perpendicular cliffs of solid glass; I picked up several small blocks for paperweights, but unluckily lost them. The range extends for probably 1,500 feet, and the height may be 250 or 300 feet.

A little farther on we came to the "Lake of the Woods." On this lake is a beaver-dam and house, and there are said to be a few beavers about there, but I have met with no one who has seen them. On the lake were large flocks of wild geese and ducks. The interest of this Park is somewhat diminished by the distance one has to travel from one remarkable point to another. After passing "The Lake of the Woods" we must have travelled about fifteen miles or more, wholly through a green pine forest, over hill and down dale, but all pine. Then we came to "Norris Hot Springs and Geysers." Here we found a number of boiling and bubbling hot springs; some send up small jets, others are great lakes of boiling water. One, called "The Emerald," is a circular hole of perhaps thirty feet in circumference. The water is of the clearest emerald green, so transparent that one could see right down into it for many yards. Within a few feet was another hot spring of quite a different character. In this the stuff that bubbled up was of a thick leaden colour; others were pouring forth streams of red, green, and yellow, all pervaded with a strong smell of sulphur. A spring called "The Paint Pot" is a great cauldron of perhaps 150 feet in circumference. On one side the deposit thrown out is of a bright salmon colour. This is a lake of pure creamy boiling paint, like liquid plaster of Paris.

After lunching in a temporary hotel, consisting of several tents, we drove on till we came to "The Fairy Falls," which can only be seen by following a steep path down the side of the cañon—a difficult path, but quite worth taking. Shortly afterwards we came upon a scene which probably cannot be paralleled on this earth. They call it, not inappropriately, "Hell's Half-acre." Here our coachman turned out of the road on to a wide expanse of white, chalky formation, which seemed to me like the upper crust of an immense honeycomb; out of this bubbled innumerable small and large hot springs. Driving over this great crust, which

"THE FAIRY FALLS."

covered a boiling lake, struck me as being rather risky, for I could see no reason why it might not give way under the weight of a coach and four at any moment. Suddenly we came upon a great opening which had fallen in. Just imagine an apple-pie a dozen acres in size, and on it you come suddenly upon a place where half an acre or so has been cut out with a knife ; or you may picture the crust as having fallen in. The coach drives close up to the edge of this place, and you look down upon a great roaring, boiling cauldron at least half an acre in size, sending up great rolls of sulphurous steam hundreds of feet into the air.[1] The terror of it is quite indescribable. I was glad when the coach got back on the hard road again. The boiling water is of a most brilliant transparent green, and it boils up great globes of various coloured gems like potatoes in a pot.

Last week, a wild duck flying over the scalding steam was sucked into the cauldron

[1] Lord Dunraven says, "The crust feels as if it might break through at any moment and drop you into fire and flames beneath, and the animals tread gingerly upon it. . . . It is dangerous ground ; I have not heard of any accident up to this time ; no modern Korah, Dathan, and Abiram as yet have been engulfed alive ; but the visits to these regions have been, like those of angels, few and far between."

and immediately shot out again cooked and ready for table—so said our coachman. As to the cooking there can be no question, for the temperature is over 200°.

Passing along Fire Hole River, we could see at intervals small and large springs, boiling hot, rising right out of the banks of the river. So you see how perfectly practicable it is to catch a fish in the river and cook it in the boiling water without moving a yard.

On we went till we came to the Lower Geyser Springs, and after a look at them, we drove on to the hotel at the Upper Geysers, completing a distance of fifty-eight miles. We had been jolted on the stage since seven o'clock in the morning. This is the scene of the Great Geysers, and one of them, called the "Riverside," which flings itself up at intervals of twenty-four hours, did us the honour of starting just as we came to it; it springs from the banks of the river, where the bridge spans it, and made a grand display for us as we crossed over.

Close by the hotel is another marvellous geyser, which, from his extreme punctuality, has earned the name of "Old Faithful." He rises once every sixty-five minutes to a second.[1] We walked up over the lava, or chalky bed, to examine his abode. There we could look down into the circular crater, from which jets of steam were rising, and great agitated bubbles of water were struggling to

"THE RIVERSIDE."

get free. Presently, without a minute's warning, up shot an enormous column of boiling

[1] When Lord Dunraven saw "Old Faithful," ten or eleven years ago, his time was "every three-quarters of an hour." The landlord now quotes it as I have stated, and he is confirmed by my own observation; but we only saw him twice.

water, it may be six feet in diameter, straight into the sky, a hundred and fifty feet or more, then spread out into a beautiful vase-like shape, and came down in hot showers all round. Of course we managed to get outside the range of the spray, but we had some difficulty in steering clear of the little rivers of hot water which were streaming all round us. The eruption lasts for about five minutes.

We saw " Old Faithful's " performances just as the sun was setting most brilliantly over the far-off western mountains. There are scores of other geysers continually bubbling, boiling, and seething on this great white plain, which is hemmed in on all sides by pine or fir-clad hills, forming a scene not to be described by me. The principal geysers have all names attached to them. "The Giantess" only shows off her powers once in fourteen days. Then there are " The Castle," " The Lion," " The Lioness," and her two cubs, " The Grand," " The Comet," &c. One of the most curious and eccentric is called " The Bee-Hive." She is very uncertain in her movements; but when she does go off she throws a strange, solid column of water straight up

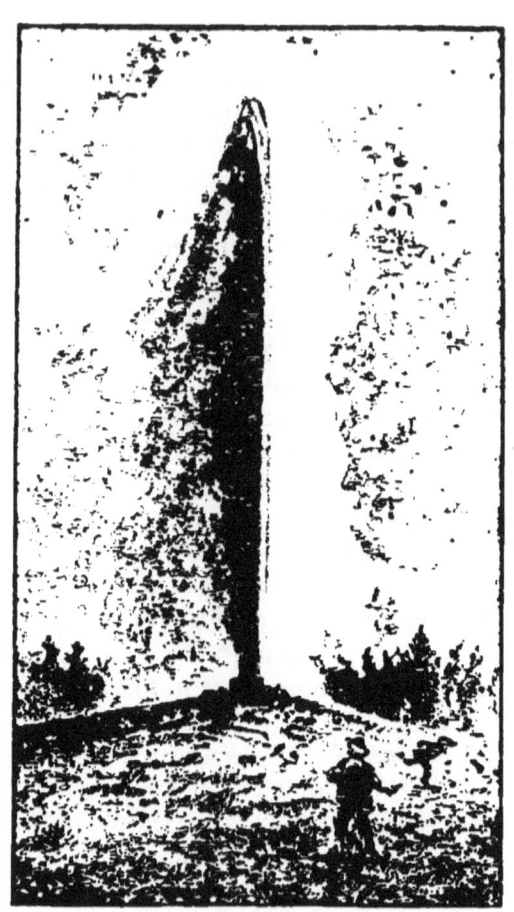
"OLD FAITHFUL."

into the air for 220 feet, which is then diffused in brilliant colours, like rockets at a Crystal Palace display of fireworks. We did not see her—her times are irregular; but there is a small one at her foot called "The Indicator," which, when it goes off, gives half an hour's warning that "The Bee-Hive" is coming. Then there is a strange commotion at the hotel, for she sometimes bursts out at midnight. A watchman on the look-out shouts, "The Bee-Hive! the Bee-Hive!" and people rush out of their beds wrapped up in blankets, or whatever clothing they can find, and off they go; there is no time to dress, for the grand display is as brief as it is magnificent.

We could not give time (two days or more) to travel fifty miles farther in order to see the grandest scene of all in this park of wonders—the Grand Cañon. I am told by everyone who has seen it that it is quite impossible by words or paint-brush to give any idea of its grandeur.

As, however, any description of the Park which omits the GRAND CAÑON would be like omitting Hamlet from the play, I will give you this quotation from Professor F. V. Haydon's report to Congress:—

"No language can do justice to the wonderful grandeur and beauty of the cañon below the lower falls, the very nearly vertical walls slightly sloping down to the water's edge on either side, so that from the summit the river appears like a thread of silver foaming over its rocky bottom; the variegated colours of the sides—yellow, red, brown, white—all intermixed and shading into each other; the gothic columns of every form standing out from the sides of the walls with greater variety and more striking colours than ever adorned a work of human art.... A celebrated artist exclaimed, with a kind of regretful enthusiasm, that these beautiful tints were beyond the reach of human art.... After the waters of the Yellowstone roll over the upper descent, they flow over the apparently flat rocky bottom ... until near the lower falls, where the channel contracts, and the waters seem to gather themselves into one compact mass, and plunge over the descent of 350 feet in detached drops of foam as white as snow, some of the larger globules of water shooting down like the contents of an exploded rocket. It is a sight far more beautiful, though not so grand or impressive as that of Niagara Falls."

The next morning we started back again by another route, on the other side of the Fire Hole River, and when we came opposite to

"Hell's Half-acre," we saw great streams of boiling sulphur water pouring down the rocks from the cauldron I have already mentioned, into the river, where I am told the boiling water runs alongside the cold a long distance before mixing with it. The fish to be found in this and other lakes and rivers in the Park are quite uneatable, being wormy, and sulphurous in flavour.

I am aware that I have utterly failed to convey anything like an adequate picture of what I have seen myself in this "region of wonder, terror, and delight." The geysers are said far to surpass both in number and in size those of Iceland or New Zealand.

I must leave it to others to explain the physical causes which produce these phenomena. It is said by the learned that the entire region was, at a comparatively recent geological period, the scene of remarkable volcanic activity, and that its last stages are visible in these hot springs and geysers.

At present the roads are, for the most part, terribly rough and unformed; but the government is active, and the work already done, both on the roads and bridges, is admirable. Sixteen miles of splendid roads had already been completed on the route we travelled over. The hotel accommodation cannot be commended. The food one gets is simply execrable; but doubtless all this will soon be changed. I am told that a wealthy company has now obtained leases for hotels, and the public may hope next year to be better fed and better lodged than they have been in the past. The hotel charges at present are four dollars a day.

The stage-coaches are not bad, and the teams are for the most part excellent. The drivers are very intelligent, civil fellows, and when once stirred up they tell most amusing stories.

The proprietors employ about two hundred and fifty horses in the Park, and as we left on the last day of the season, I was curious to know what became of the horses during the winter. I was told that they are all turned loose on the prairie, to paw up their living from under the snow on the foothills where it lies thin, and in the spring they are brought in fatter and stronger than when they went out.

Now that nearly all the buffaloes in the country have been killed, very strict game laws have been put in force for their preser-

vation. I am told that within the Park there is now very little game of any kind. A man was recently fined 100 dollars and costs and imprisoned for six months for killing two elk and eight beaver within the Park, whilst a premium of ten dollars is given for the destruction of a bear.

Let me add that there is some capital trout fishing in the Yellowstone River, just outside the Park, and we had made arrangements to spend a day there and to sleep at "Yankee Jim's," who keeps a small inn by the riverside. Jim is a well-known character throughout the country, but our experience of him did not encourage us to take up our abode in his little shanty. When sober we are told he is a highly respectable character; but when drunk (and he happened to be in that condition when we made his acquaintance) he is a madman, and a spiritualist able to see through mountains, to boot. On the whole, we did not care to cultivate Jim's acquaintance, so we had to give up our day's fishing in the Yellowstone. We may do better by-and-by in the West Gallatin River.

Just before sundown, and as we were passing through "The Golden Gate," I saw a pedestrian coming up the road at a rapid pace. I was sitting on the box-seat, and I said to the driver—

"Where can yonder fellow be going in this

direction at this time of day; there is not a house of any kind within twenty miles?" "It is curious," said he.

When we came up to the pedestrian, "By Jove! it's Frank!" I shouted. "Pull up, driver! Jump up, my boy!" He was looking strong and well, and almost as brown as a red Indian, and he soon explained to me the mystery of my not hearing from him. He had sent a telegram to Chicago, which I never received, requesting me to go straight on to Bozeman, and he had driven in to Bozeman five days successively, twenty-four miles each day, to meet us, and of course was as much bewildered about me as I had been about him. The passenger agent at Bozeman had put wrong initials on the telegram I had sent from St. Paul, and the post-master had refused to give it up for two or three days; when by chance Frank met the passenger agent, who told him about the telegram and explained his mistake to the post-master. At last he got the message, and he then started off at once for Livingston and the Park, and met us coming out of it, instead of accompanying us through it, as I had planned.

128 *MY HOLIDAY IN THE ROCKIES.*

In due time we reached Bozeman, and by seven o'clock in the evening of the day after our first meeting we were safely housed in Frank's little log hut.

LETTER No. XIII.

Livingston to Bozeman—Bozeman City—Arrival at Frank's ranche—Frank's progress—The shanty—Kitten and mice—Aroused by a ground squirrel—Variation of climate—A snowstorm—Our beds drenched—"Baching" it—Shaving under difficulties—Situation—Fertility of the soil—Cultivation of strawberries—Fine grazing district—Climate—Story of our holiday on the ranche—Fishing in West Gallatin river—New bridge and old canoe—"The coloured aristocracy"—Three bear stories.

Frank's Ranche, Oct., 1885.

HE railroad from Livingston to Bozeman runs through very picturesque scenery, and after a steep grade of 116 feet to the mile, passes through a tunnel in the mountain at an elevation of 5,565 feet above the ocean. The train then runs down the western slope through a remarkably grand cañon, and passes

K

out into the broad valley of West Gallatin; in a few minutes more Bozeman is reached.

This delightful little city of about 3,000 inhabitants is seated on the East Gallatin

CAÑON NEAR BOZEMAN.

river at the eastern end of the Gallatin Valley, and is the county seat of Gallatin. It has a fine court house, three hotels, a fine opera house, seven public halls, five churches, and two well-conducted newspapers.

The streets are well laid out, and there are many very fine, handsome buildings in the town, and pretty villas in its suburbs.

Unfortunately, time did not admit of my making any stay in the town, or of calling upon persons to whom I had introductions; it was necessary to hurry on to get to Frank's ranche before dark. We hired a handsome waggonette, and, with a spanking pair of horses, we drove along a perfectly level well-trodden road across the prairie for twelve miles, and eventually pulled up at Frank's mansion while there was light enough to enable us to see it, but not to criticise it too severely.

Here, then, at last, after nearly six weeks of hard travelling by sea and land, I had reached the chief goal of my journey.

I have already taken you so completely into my confidence by telling you of Frank's disasters and misfortunes, that it is but fair to him that I should now describe to you his small successes; not that he has very much to show at present, but he seems to me to be on the right track. He already possesses by homestead right 160 acres of very good land, which will be absolutely his freehold in two years' time; he also owns a hundred acres of good railroad feeding land on the foothills; he has fenced round the whole of this with strong posts, rails, and barbed wire; he has built himself a log hut; he has purchased a fair set of agricultural implements, including wagons, and a handsome buggie; he has a pair of strong horses, a number of pigs, some poultry, and a few cows and calves; he has a well-stocked garden, which produces all the vegetables he requires, and he has laid down about half an acre of land with strawberries: next summer this will produce a large crop.

When I remind you that he has acquired this little property with only trifling assistance from me, and mainly by the labour of his own hands, in the space of three years, you will understand that I am inspired with some hopes for his future.

Frank's shanty originally consisted of one room nineteen feet by seventeen, but in anticipation of his visitors, he and B. built an additional room of about the same size. The old room having a boarded floor was breakfast, dining, drawing-room, and library com-

FRANK'S CABIN, FROM A SKETCH BY HIMSELF.

bined, and was also the visitors' bedroom. Our beds were made upon planks laid upon four logs, and consisted of a bundle of straw laid on the planks, a blanket on the straw, and a couple of rugs to roll ourselves in. These beds were placed one on each side of the room, and when bed-time came, a cotton curtain was suspended across the middle, and thus each lodger had a bedroom to himself.

Our beds being those usually occupied by Frank and his friend, they rigged up for themselves a sort of long manger or bunk in the new (or kitchen) compartment, and slept in it feet to feet.

I cannot boast that I slept soundly under these novel circumstances. The first night Frank's kitten was left in the room to scare the mice away, and proved to be a greater nuisance than the mice; the next night she was excluded, and I was aroused out of my sleep by a crash among some empty bottles. I struck a light, and after searching about for some time, I caught sight of a little ground squirrel which had come in through a hole in the floor. The next night I was aroused by this little wretch running over my face in a playful mood, and I sat up slipper in hand for over an hour waiting for a chance to fling it at him, but he did not afford me one. This little squirrel and a few mice were our only troubles; otherwise we should have slept quite as comfortably as in our own beds at home.

The weather during the first six days and nights had been most delightful, very hot by day and pleasantly cool by night; on the seventh and last night of our stay, the thermometer, by way of giving us a taste of the variation of climate here, suddenly dropped from 78° to 34°, and snow and rain fell all night. This wintry blast is always looked for just at this time, and lasts for about twenty-four hours; then the Indian summer resumes its reign till far on into November. Months of dry and very hot weather had dried the mud covering of the shanty into powder, and when my friend M. awoke in the morning, he found that the roof above him had proved a sieve, and he and his bed were thoroughly soaked. I had fared only a little better; but we didn't mind these trifling inconveniences. I found my umbrella very useful to sit under at breakfast, and M. managed very well when wrapped up in his macintosh.

Frank and his friend had, from long practice, acquired the art of baking and cooking to perfection. While the one lighted the

SHAVING OUTSIDE THE CABIN.

stove, made the hot cakes, and broiled the bacon, the other started off to milk the cow and collect some new-laid eggs—the result being an excellent and plentiful breakfast, eaten with the splendid appetite due to abundant exercise on these health-giving hills.

Whilst these preparations were going on M. and I washed by turns; our basin was a miner's old iron washpan, and our shaving operations were performed outside.

Dinner demanded greater efforts, to which our hosts proved quite equal. They roast, boil, and stew to perfection, and make very nice puddings. There is but one glass tumbler in the establishment, so we drank pure water out of teacups; of these there are four, but Frank boasts only one saucer.

In the matter of crockery I am sorry to say Frank was sadly deficient; the kitten and the invading little squirrel had recently played havoc in his china closet; we managed, however, very well. We had no change of plates, but we washed them as we progressed with our meals.

I should tell you that the shanty is situated at the foot of the foothills of the mountains, and is about 5,000 feet above sea level, overlooking towards the west an expanse of level country of from twenty to thirty miles in extent; the whole circumference being the jagged ranges of the mountains. Some parts of the great plain are rather rocky and thin, but the nutritious bunch-grass grows everywhere; other parts, again, are of a deep, loamy, dark-coloured soil, which produces

LOOKING TOWARDS BOZEMAN.

crops of wheat of forty to sixty bushels to the acre year after year. All had been cut and gathered before our arrival, but we could easily see by the stacks and the stubble what the crops must have been.

Oats have been grown there this last season which reached 100 bushels to the acre.

The following sensible remarks, cut from the excellent paper I have already quoted, entirely confirm my own impression of this country:—

"This is pre-eminently the land for the poor man, but only for the poor man who is willing to work hard. He can raise enough to support his family, and if he has a few cows their increase will in the course of a few years make him well-to-do. I spent a night a short time since in the cabin of a settler who, with his wife and four children, had located about forty miles from the railroad. He had ten cows, a team of horses, and a mowing machine. From the cows his wife made enough butter to pay the living expenses of the family. He puts up hay for the stock in summer, and then hires himself out to neighbours at good wages. His calves and colts were in fine condition, and everything pointed to a most comfortable future for this sturdy, energetic settler.

"Who can tell how many families there may not be scattered over the broad West, who from similar small beginnings have attained by industry and thrift a competence, or even wealth."—*Forest and Stream.*

I was so well pleased with the absolute truthfulness of Frank's reports, and satisfied with the progress he had made, that I was glad to place him in a position to acquire an adjoining ranche of 250 acres, so that he may now be said to possess a capital farm of 500 acres, capable of carrying at a moderate computation fifty head of cattle, ten pigs, fifteen to twenty horses, and two hundred chickens. The farm includes about a hundred and fifty acres of excellent arable land, which may at a very moderate estimate be expected to produce 3,000 bushels of wheat, barley, and oats. His garden produces many marketable vegetables, and he has milk, butter, and eggs.

Strawberries grow on the land to a large size and of excellent flavour, and the half acre now planted would, it was calculated, produce a clear net profit of at least 200 dollars for the first year. Strawberries, I was told, produce from 250 to 500 bushels to the acre after the first year—say 250 bushels @ 10 cents a quart. Thirty-two quarts to bushel @ 10 cents = $3 20c. or $750 60c. an acre. Expenses of gathering, 2 cents a quart = 150 dollars; cost of cultivation, 120 dollars = 270 dollars; this deducted from product, $750 60c., leaves net profit $480—say £100 sterling.

Strawberries are too perishable to be conveyed a long distance, but the immense mining population in the vicinity can consume all that can be grown. In course of time strawberry jam may be made here, and sent even to England, to compete with the English farmer in the new article of commerce which Mr. Gladstone has suggested for him.

Frank's neighbour McD. has planted a number of apple and other fruit trees in and around his garden, and these young trees are thriving, and give promise in a year or two of bearing much fruit. Frank's land is equally suited for similar trees.

On the whole, it appears to me that Frank has now only to go on with the same dogged perseverance he has hitherto shown, and he will soon be in a very comfortable position, and make up for his early losses in Minnesota. I should add that the farm is well watered by a perpetual little stream which runs down from the mountains, and never freezes or diminishes.

This district has the reputation of being the best grazing country in the world. Cattle rarely require any other food during the winter than what the native grasses supply. The bunch-grass grows abundantly, not only in the valleys and on the benches, but on the foothills and mountain slopes. Cattle do not require housing in the winter, but are foddered sometimes, or rather allowed to browse round the straw-stacks. Horses maintain themselves by pawing up the snow as the reindeer do in Northern Europe.

The climate of Montana is peculiarly mild considering its altitude; this is doubtless owing to the influence of the great warm Japan current of the Pacific Ocean and the prevailing westerly Chinook wind. This warm pleasant breeze was distinctly perceptible by us as we ascended the hills, even in the then hot weather. The atmosphere is singularly dry, pure, and exhilarating, and this is especially the case on the spot where Frank has chosen his location. They never have the bitter cold "blizzards" which one hears of in other states and territories; and when the thermometer stands at 20°, 30°, and even 45° below zero, as it sometimes does in the winter months, the cold is endurable.

Now let me give you a little history of our short "Holiday in the Rockies."

Sunday.—There being no church or place

of worship of any kind, I regret to say, within many miles, we had to content ourselves with some quiet reading at home. The Church Missionary Societies should look after these boys scattered about here and there in these mountain wilds. The day was calm and bright, but by no means cool; the thermometer stood at 125° in the sun. In the afternoon we walked a considerable distance in the shade of the cañon, and then somewhat foolishly scrambled up one side of it in order to make a short cut over the mountain towards home, and a risky climb it was; but on reaching the top we were rewarded by a fine new view of the whole valley.

There is a remarkable echo up this cañon, equal, I have no doubt, to that celebrated one at Killarney which, if asked " How do you do, Paddy Blake?" will answer " Pretty well, I thank you."

Monday we walked up the foothills to look for some grouse and prairie chickens to shoot, but could not see any, greatly to my friend M.'s disappointment; he had come well provided with ammunition, both for large and small game. Unfortunately our time did not admit of very extended wanderings in search of sport. We then called upon neighbour McD., an old rancher who has had many rough experiences, and who tells long stories of perils he had undergone in the early Californian gold diggings and in fights with Indians. On his ranche he has built a nice little house, of which I made the accompanying sketch. A

NEIGHBOUR McD.'S COTTAGE.

house of this description, of wood planking, comprising two good-sized rooms and a kitchen on the ground floor, and two bedrooms, can be built for about 250 dollars.

He compelled us to stay to dinner. His wife, an active good-looking Canadian body, bustled about and prepared us an excellent dinner of hashed chicken, sweet cakes, coffee, and apple tart. She waited upon us at table and urged us to eat, and was pleased to see with what excellent appetites we fell to. She was gratified at the well-merited praise we lavished on her cooking.

After dinner, we had what I may call a musical evening. Frank gave us some songs, and his friend accompanied him on the guitar.

On *Tuesday* we drove for fifteen miles across the prairie to the West Gallatin River, where I was told good fishing may be had. We stayed at a comfortable hotel which had no licence for strong drinks, and we had to content ourselves with tea and coffee.

We immediately started for the river—a really fine stream, well stocked with trout and other fish. You already know something of my enthusiasm, as well as my bad luck, in matters piscatorial. I caught no trout, but you will perhaps be surprised to hear I brought home half-a-dozen half-pound fish called "White fish." I caught these with a large black fly with a red body. The fish takes this fly freely, but he has no pluck whatever; no sooner is he hooked than he succumbs at once, and one has nothing to do but pull him out of the water—there is no sport or fight in him. Our jolly landlord had taken us to a favourite spot, where he himself fished with a pole and twine, sitting on the stump of a tree;

> "There sat my friend with patient skill,
> Attending of his trembling quill."
> Sir H. Wotton.

FISHING IN THE WEST GALLATIN.

he baited his hook with grasshoppers and locusts, and with this bait he was usually very successful, but on that particular evening he caught nothing, and soon gave up.

My own success had so much surprised me that next morning I was up at six o'clock, and had caught six more white fish before breakfast.

They were cooked for us, and certainly if they afford poor sport, they are very pleasant, delicate eating. I cannot honestly take much credit to myself for these feats. Our hostess, a very severe hard-featured Calvinistic person, took all the conceit out of me at once by solemnly telling the company at the breakfast table that she could go down to the river and catch as many white fish as she wanted with a worm hooked on to a pin.

I was reminded of the angler in "The Sketch Book":—

"I recollect that after toiling and watching and creeping about . . . with scarcely any success, in spite of all our admirable apparatus, a lubberly country urchin came down from the hills with a rod made from a branch of a tree, a few yards of twine, and, as Heaven shall help me! I believe a crooked pin for a hook, baited with a vile earthworm—and in half-an-hour caught more fish than we had nibbles throughout the day!"

Our host, a wealthy rancher as well as innkeeper, was of a more jovial turn, especially when he was not awed by the presence of his austere wife. He had been a slave-owner in pre-emancipation days, and so had his fathers before him; and he vowed the niggers were far better off then than they are now. "God Almighty," said he, "made the niggers black and unthrifty, and do what you will you can never make them anything else. The utmost height of a nigger's ambition is to drive a coach or to be a waiter in an hotel; and it is just all he is good for."

This reminded me of the many members of the "coloured aristocracy" I had met with as waiters at hotels and in railroad dining-cars. I remember one especially—the head-boss of a small army of black waiters at one of the largest hotels in an Eastern city—a tall portly fellow in evening dress, diamond shirt studs, and white kid gloves. He stands at the entrance of the saloon, and receives the guests with a dignified bend and a patronizing wave of his hand which my Lord Mayor at a grand reception could not surpass. We, unshaven and dust-stained travellers, were quite awed in his presence, as he loftily passed us on to another diamond-studded and gold-chained nigger, who condescended to find us a table. We soon learned that if you expect to get any decent attention from a negro, you had better slip a "quarter" into his ready and expectant palm ; then he will wait upon you quickly and well. Pay him beforehand, and he will serve you in anticipation of further tips—a quarter in hand is worth to him a good deal more than a possible dollar in the end, which may never come.

These negro waiters generally speak good Yankee English ; they don't say " Massa ; " and if one may judge by the eagerness with which they will lean over one's shoulder to peruse a letter one may be writing or reading, I suppose they have been tolerably well educated. Here is an account of an aristocratic wedding cut from a Southern paper :—

"A wedding took place in South Carolina recently, the bride belonging to one of the oldest families of the coloured aristocracy and the groom being presumably a man of means and evidently of much respectability. When the fateful question was asked by the officiating clergyman (also coloured) it was thus translated by him, possibly with an eye to the intensely respectable nature of the whole affair : ' N., wilt thou have this lady to be thy wedded wife?' &c., and the blushing bride, when her turn came, was asked if she would have 'this young gentleman.'"

We returned across the prairie on *Wednesday* morning, noting as we passed that the whole route was dotted here and there with substantial farmhouses; some of these were large and handsome, surrounded by buildings as good and substantial-looking as any to be seen in the old country.

The West Gallatin is all very well if one's only object in fishing is to catch fish, but I would rather have one day on the pleasant " Dove," with only a brace of trout in my creél, or, indeed, without any trout at all, than a hundred days on the brown prairie-bound banks of the Gallatin with creels full of the stupid white fish. I want buttercups and daisies, water-ouzels, king-fishers, green meadows, and the songs of birds when "I go a-fishing."

On passing over the new bridge we saw an old Indian canoe rotting and half hidden in the mud. If I were given to moralizing, "the new bridge and the old canoe" should form a melancholy theme; but I will leave my readers to compose it for themselves.

Frank's companion B. being of an inquiring mind, knew every farm and every farmer on the route, or perhaps in the whole valley. He knew the value of every man's estate, and how he stood with his banker; one was worth 50,000 dollars, another 20,000, and here and there an unthrifty "Rip Van Winkle" with an insuperable aversion to labour and hopelessly in debt. Amongst them were one or two millionaires. It is a characteristic of this community that everyone knows to a dollar how much everyone else is worth. Generally they seemed to be well-to-do and thriving; and when I looked at the numerous great ricks of wheat, the abundant stubble, the rich dark soil so easily and so cheaply cultivated, and the cattle and horses around, it was plain to my perception that a man of ordinary industry, intelligence, and thrift must inevitably become not merely well-to-do, but wealthy.

Thursday.—B. drove into town for our letters, but found none. By this time our fresh meat had given out, so Frank and M.

went out and ran down a couple of chickens. Frank chopped their heads off, plucked, and roasted them very deftly. It was an excessively hot day, the thermometer standing at 125° in the sun. I remained indoors most of the day clearing off my correspondence, and in the evening we compared notes as to Frank's past adventures and future prospects.

Friday.—This being our last day, I wandered up the creek in the morning, and gathered a few wild flowers of bright hues, and packed them up to carry home. Of course the time for flowers is all but over now, but I am told that in the summer-time the whole hillside is ablaze with small wild roses and other flowers.

In the afternoon we had intended to do a little mountain climbing. We had gone a mile on the road to ascend Ross's Peak, a mountain (of which I made a sketch) about 10,000 feet above sea level, and at a distance of about seven miles; but on looking towards the mountains in the west we noticed that the bright sunshine in which we were walking was obscured in their direction by heavy, suspicious clouds. And presently a few drops fell. Before we could get back to our cabin the rain came down in torrents, with thunder and lightning; and, looking up to Ross's Peak, we found that he had already assumed his winter mantle of snow. This is the first rain we have had since our arrival in America, and as it was our last day we were sorry to

ROSS'S PEAK.

miss the fine view to be obtained from the peak. The ascent, we were told, was in fine weather not difficult, though no doubt very laborious. In the evening the western mountains across the valley presented a very interesting appearance. They were now clad with snow, and a thick black cloud hung just above them, leaving a clear-cut outline of white peaks; the sunset was glowing like a great fiery furnace behind them. It was a splendid sight.

Before night set in the thermometer had fallen from 78° in the shade, as it stood in the morning, to 34°, and during the night we had the deluge which I have already mentioned. To-morrow we start on our homeward journey.

I told you in my first letter that it was my intention to spend my holiday in this region, and here I am sitting in our little log cabin, overlooking a vast expanse of prairie valley, nearly six thousand miles away from my native land. So much of one's time is taken up in the railway trains that little is left for doing anything out of them. I told you that the three special horrors I expected to have to encounter would be mosquitoes, Indians, and bears! I saw one or two mosquitoes in New York, and I *felt* them in Chicago, but only slightly; the season is over for these pests, but the present unusual weather stirs up a few now and then. As for Indians, I have only seen a few wigwams and one or two horsemen, perfectly peaceable and friendly now, though a few years ago this Gallatin Valley was the scene of many a bloody engagement between them and the settlers, and old-timers have long tales to tell of many terrible affrays. Nor have I yet met with a grizzly, though there are plenty of these fellows, as well as "silver tips" and black bears, up in the mountains.

Last week a big black bear came down through this ranche and found his way to a slaughter-house in the neighbourhood of Bozeman, where he was discovered amusing himself by tearing about the offal. Two butchers in town armed themselves with a couple of rusty old rifles, and starting off on a moonlight night, kept watch for Master Bruin's appearance. Eventually they spied him on the top of the roof of the slaughter-house (a by no means easy roof to get on). They put two balls into him, and he rolled over dead. His skin was being exhibited in Bozeman as we passed through.

While I am on the subject of bears, I may as well tell you another tale just as an eyewitness told it to me.

A few weeks ago a party of miners, returning home after prospecting all summer, were encamped in a fine hunting-ground, up in the mountains near Ross's Peak, lately the favourite resort of Flat-head Indians. They started one morning on a deer and elk hunt, and having separated to scare out the game, one of them suddenly came upon a great grizzly basking in the sun in front of his den. The bear allowed him to approach within a few yards, being apparently in a drowsy state, and the hunter, being a "tenderfoot" (new-comer), did not take the ordinary precautions which experience teaches; but thinking all the bear stories he had ever heard were mere twaddle, imprudently fired in the animal's face, breaking his jaw. This at once aroused the fury of Bruin, and he rushed on the hunter, who succeeded in planting another ball in his shoulder, but this failed to stop him. Being now at such close quarters that another shot was impossible, he tried to jam his rifle down the bear's throat; they then became locked together in a deadly struggle. After wrestling for a few seconds, both hunter and bear fell over a log and down a steep ravine.

At this juncture, a dog belonging to one of the party, hearing the row, came up barking, and distracted the bear's attention; the hunter thus succeeded in escaping from the deadly hug and regained his rifle, the stock of which had been split in the first struggle. The bear then started off, feeling, no doubt, that with a broken jaw and a dislocated shoulder the odds were against him. The hunter renewed the chase, and being now joined by the rest of his party, they followed the quarry in this wounded state for eight miles, and eventually killed him.

A short time prior to this incident a man and a boy were up in a cañon a few miles to the north, cutting cord-wood. The man saw a cinnamon bear, and fired at him, wounding him in the shoulder. The bear turned on him; and the man having no more ammunition—it being in the boy's charge—threw down his rifle and scrambled up the nearest tree; the bear rushed up after him, caught hold of his leg, and tore his boot off, at the same time tearing the flesh of his leg open to the bone. The man then succeeded in getting beyond the bear's reach.

Bruin then turned his attention to the boy, who was manfully engaged in reloading

"THE BEAR TORE HIS FOOT OFF."

the rifle. He seized and hugged the lad, and, being on a steep incline, the two rolled over and over till they came to the bottom of the mountain, where the bear left his victim for dead, and then returned to the man, who was still treed. Probably feeling some stiffness from the wound in his shoulder, he could no longer climb, but having amused the man in the tree by leisurely walking round and round it for three or four hours, he then quietly departed.

It fortunately turned out that the boy was not killed, but terribly shaken. He eventually recovered from the fearful ordeal he had undergone.

These bear stories may be taken as facts, and as substantial proofs that, although we luckily did not encounter any bears, there are plenty of them up in the hills just above us.

LETTER No. XIV.

Saying "Goodbye"—Departure in a heavy snowstorm—Gallatin Valley—Helena—Garrison—Butte City—Salt Lake City—Polygamy—Articles of faith—Trial of a murderer—Trial of polygamists.

Cheyenne, Wyoming, Oct., 1885.

N Saturday morning we found the ground covered with snow, and it was bitterly cold. It seemed as if this sudden change had come upon us opportunely to prevent our carrying away a too favourable impression of the climate. Truly, the day was a rough one, and we had to drive twelve miles across the prairie to Bozeman in a blinding storm of snow and sleet, and over a road smooth and level a week ago, but now full of holes and deep ruts up to the axles. Our progress through the sludgy snow was very slow.

I had hoped to make some calls in Bozeman, but the weather prevented my doing so.

We reached the station only just in time to catch the train for Helena, and we were not sorry to get under cover from the pitiless storm.

Now the time had arrived for saying goodbye to the boy I had gone so far to see, a great lump came into my throat as I thought of the years that may pass before we meet again; of his rough journey back, and of the poor little leaky shanty he had to winter in, and to which he had voluntarily exiled himself.

But for this taste of wintry weather, I should have left Frank's ranche with a more cheerful heart, yet with a false impression of the country and climate.

Unquestionably the life on a ranche such as Frank's is a rough and hard one, and I should be sorry if I have said anything throughout this narrative that might induce any aspiring youth to adopt a similar mode of life under a contrary impression. But for a young fellow who is willing to banish himself from all society and to work as Frank has done, I can certainly commend this country.

We left Bozeman in the afternoon for Helena and Garrison, the junction where we turn to the south on the Branch Line of the Union Pacific.

As I felt a special and peculiar interest in the beautiful Gallatin Valley, it was some disappointment to me that my latest view of it was in the midst of a heavy snowstorm. Our railroad route ran for thirty miles through this valley, and had the afternoon been clear, we might have caught a last glimpse of the little log cabin ten miles away up yonder, at the foot of the Eastern Hills.

At the head of the valley we came to "Gallatin City." Here "The Gallatin," "The Madison," and "Jefferson" rivers are lost in the great Missouri. After crossing the Missouri, the road passes down the Missouri Valley to Helena. No sooner had we got out of the valley than the storm cleared off, the evening sun shone out brightly, and by the time we arrived at Helena, just 100 miles from Bozeman, we found ourselves again in the same mild, genial atmosphere we had experienced previous to the storm. No snow had fallen at Helena.

Helena, the capital of Montana, has a population of 8,000, is situated at the eastern foot of the main chain of the Rockies, and close to the famous "Last Chance" gold mines, out of which $10,000,000 worth of gold has been taken, and which still yields a considerable amount annually. This circumstance, and the fact that it is the nearest point in the mining region to the head of navigation on the Missouri river at Fort Benton, gave Helena a great start in earlier days, and it is certainly likely to maintain its position as the chief commercial town of Montana territory. It is surrounded by mountains, rising one above the other, till the more distant are lost in the clouds, forming a view of striking beauty and grandeur.

The town itself, so far as we had time to observe, is not well built; the streets are narrow, crooked, and steep; but it has all the appearance of wealth and prosperity. It has four national banks, a fine opera house, seating 1,200, and two daily papers. The shops are large, and full of attractive-looking "stock." The city is lighted by the Brush electric light system.

The hotel we stopped at is very large and very comfortable, but they won't black one's boots. If you wish to indulge in this luxury you must descend to the boot-black's quarters, and mount on his stool. He will polish you off in five minutes, and scorns anything less than a shilling for doing it. Why should he take less when he finds full employment all the day long at this rate of pay? I reckoned that fellow was making thirty shillings a day by his blacking.

Next morning we started for Garrison. The route from Helena to "The Mullan Pass" is most picturesque, taking us through the charming valley of "Prickly Pear," and past great masses of craggy rocks and boulders. "The Mullan Pass" takes us over, or rather through the main range of the Rocky Mountains by a tunnel 3,850 feet in length, and at an elevation above sea-level of 5,547 feet.

Now we are at Garrison, where we leave

the Great Northern Pacific Railway, on which we have travelled so pleasantly over 1,200 miles of country, through scenes as tame and scenes as wildly picturesque as are probably to be found in any other part of this great country.

Our route now lies due south for a distance of nearly 500 miles to Ogden and Salt Lake City.

The cars being narrow gauge, we did not find them so pleasant as those we had just left; but as we secured sleeping compartments, and the passengers for part of the way were few, we had nothing to complain of. On this line there are no dining-cars, so we had to descend at various stations for scrambling meals, at not by any means nice hotels.

At a distance of about thirty miles from Garrison, we passed the great mining city of Butte, on the west side of the main dividing range of the Rocky Mountains; for an hour or two our car was crowded with holiday people from that wealthy city, decked out very gorgeously, and proud of their display of jewellery. Butte is a city of 18,000 inhabitants, and is called "a mining camp."

It is the county seat of Silver Bow county. There are over 1,300 patented mines in this district, five smelters, and nine quartz mills. The mines produce silver, copper, and gold, the shipments of which amount to $6,000,000 annually. The adjoining city of Anaconda, which two years ago consisted of two tents, has now 3,000 inhabitants, and boasts of having the largest smelter in the world. It cost a million dollars, and the two owners are said to be worth forty million dollars each— they own two mines. This smelter pays the Union Pacific a hundred thousand dollars a month for carrying ore over a little branch line of nine miles in length.

The train passes through the Cache Valley, which is fifty miles long and ten miles broad; it is wholly occupied by Mormons. On the south-east side of the valley is the city of Logan, where a fine temple overlooking the whole of the valley has been built. There are seventeen separate settlements in this most fertile valley, and these, seen from the railway, look like green patches of verdure dotted over the great brown prairie, each settlement being hidden in groves of green trees.

We reached Ogden at 5.30 p.m., and took train the same evening for Salt Lake City, where we arrived at the Walker House Hotel at eight.

Salt Lake City.

A residence of one day and two nights in Salt Lake City does not constitute me an authority or entitle me to put forth any opinions on the vexed question of Mormonism, but as I chanced to reach the city in stirring times, I venture to give two or three quotations from the current literature, which exhibit the question in its two aspects. The first is an extract from a very well-written pamphlet by Mrs. H. M. Whitney *in favour of* Polygamy. She says:—

"I have been a spectator and a participator in this order of matrimony for over thirty years, and, being a first wife, I have had every opportunity for judging in regard to its merits. The Scriptures declare, 'By their fruits ye shall know them;' so I know that this system tends to promote and preserve social purity, and that this alone can remedy the great social evils of the present day. When lived up to as the Lord designed it should be, it will exalt the human family; and those who have entered into it with pure motives, and continue to practise it in righteousness, can testify to the truth of these statements. There are real and tangible blessings enjoyed under this system which cannot be obtained in any other way. Not only can the cares and burdens be equally distributed among the members of the family, but they can assist one another in many ways, and if blessed with congenial natures and filled with the love of God, their souls will be expanded, and in the place of selfishness, patience and charity will find place in their hearts, driving therefrom all feelings of strife and discord."

The little *if* in the last sentence seems to beg the whole question, and reminds one of Cowper's epigram :—

"If John marries Mary, and Mary alone,
'Tis a very good match between Mary and John;
Should John wed a score, O, the claws and the scratches !
It can't be a match—it's a bundle of matches !"

Another enthusiastic lady says :—

"Shall we, the wives and daughters of the best men on earth, submit to the dictation of unholy, licentious, and wicked men? No, never! I feel that it is high time for the women of Utah to stand up and defend this Heaven-revealed principle. I am a polygamous wife, and am proud to say it. I regard those women who are my husband's wives to be so as much as I am. Our husbands are virtuous and noble men, and are the friends of all mankind."

The following is taken from the biennial message of W. M. Budd, Governor of Idaho, and, I fancy, fairly represents the general feeling of the United States Government on this very important question at this time :—

"POLYGAMOUS AND TREASONOUS MORMONISM.

"While the constitution of our nation guarantees to every person of whatever birth, rank, or condition, past or present, a generous freedom in his own thoughts and religious convictions, not only the common law pronounces against adultery, bigamy, and polygamy, but every consideration of safety urges against permitting a self-proclaimed enemy to harbour within our fold while he gathers strength to strike at our life with the venom he already possesses. It becomes you to approach the discussion of this malignant mischief, that has retarded the Territory in the past and threatens such disaster for the future, with brave and grave deliberation. If you decide after careful investigation, as I have decided, that there can be no harmony between virtue and such monstrous vice; that either—and that at no distant day—pure, moral Christianity, that is such from fear of God, love of Christ and hope of heaven, or this leprous legacy of barbarity and sensual riot must possess the land to the exclusion of the other, then I say, it is not merciful to temporize with the blow that must be struck to free this Territory of this social plague and political curse. Polygamous and treasonous Mormonism stalks wantonly, insolently, and blatantly through this Territory, to the shame and degradation of every Christian woman and every man with a love for law and a regard for decency. Crime under the guise of religion is a hundred fold worse than under the banner of Satan. The leaders, owners, and bidder of this unholy, licentious, and treasonable institution are saints to glut their own vile and selfish purposes. Selfishness, which sees in the world only a mirror just large enough to reflect itself, writes in their case, as it always has written, a story of cant, hypocrisy, falsehood, deceit, fraud, and violence; and the inevitable logic of events, which is stronger than all the sins that infamy, greed, and selfishness are heir to, will write the invariable sequel: detection, retribution, expiation, and the felon's cell. These law-breakers mock and scoff the power of this great government, abuse our free institutions, and bedraggle our flag in the muck and mire of their offences. The guilty may be brought to bay and to justice even at the time when they imagine themselves most strongly entrenched. The Mormon leaders were never more defiant than at this peculiar and particular time. I conjure you to do your utmost toward destroying the polluting practices of this seditious organization. Suppress these licentious saints with their plural marriages, and so wipe away the fetid blotch upon this Territory, that is a stench in the nostrils of all the honest humanity within our borders. I advise the enactment of such laws and amendments as shall make effective the laws of God and man regarding adultery, bigamy, and polygamy, and compel loyalty to the nation and respect for the flag."

"Articles of Faith of the Church of Jesus Christ of Latter-Day Saints.

"1. We believe in God the Eternal Father, and in His Son Jesus Christ, and in the Holy Ghost.

"2. We believe that men will be punished for their own sins, and not for Adam's transgression.

"3. We believe that through the atonement of Christ all mankind may be saved, by obedience to the laws and ordinances of the Gospel.

"4. We believe that these ordinances are: first, Faith in the Lord Jesus Christ; second, Repentance; third, Baptism by immersion for the remission of sins; fourth, Laying on of hands for the gift of the Holy Ghost.

"5. We believe that a man must be called of God by 'prophecy and by the laying on of hands,' by those who are in authority, to preach the Gospel and administer in the ordinances thereof.

"6. We believe in the same organization that existed in the primitive church, viz., apostles, prophets, pastors, teachers, evangelists, &c.

"7. We believe in the gift of tongues, prophecy, revelation, visions, healing, interpretation of tongues, &c.

"8. We believe the Bible to be the word of God,

as far as it is translated correctly; we also believe the Book of Mormon to be the Word of God.

"9. We believe all that God has revealed, all that He does now reveal, and we believe that He will yet reveal many great and important things pertaining to the Kingdom of God.

"10. We believe in the literal gathering of Israel, and in the restoration of the Ten Tribes. That Zion will be built upon this continent. That Christ will reign personally upon the earth, and that the earth will be renewed and receive its paradisiacal glory.

"11. We claim the privilege of worshipping Almighty God according to the dictates of our conscience, and allow all men the same privilege, let them worship how, where, or what they may.

"12. We believe in being subject to kings, presidents, rulers, and magistrates, in obeying, honouring, and sustaining the law.

"13. We believe in being honest, true, chaste, benevolent, virtuous, and in doing good to *all men*: indeed, we may say that we follow the admonition of Paul, 'We believe all things, we hope all things,' we have endured many things, and hope to be able to endure all things. If there is anything virtuous, lovely, or of good report or praiseworthy, we seek after these things.—JOSEPH SMITH."

This is all very well as far as it goes, but I find nothing about polygamy here, and I learn elsewhere that—

"According to Mormon theology, God the Father, the Supreme Jehovah, became man in the form of Adam, and thus became the father of the human race. He is thus represented as a being of parts such as we are. And all true and faithful Mormons who live up to their privileges, who take many wives, and who beget many children, will in the process of time become gods to all those who spring from them. Brigham Young was regarded as God by some of his followers even before his death."

In walking down Main Street I came to a great crowd opposite the court-house. I was curious to know what was going on, and to see the interior of a law court in a Mormon city, but the staircase was so completely blocked that I could not get in. On inquiry I learned that a murderer named Hopt was receiving his sentence, and that three Mormons were being tried for polygamy.

The court, in passing sentence on Hopt, said "The penalty of the crime for which you have been convicted is death, and must be inflicted by hanging you by the neck, or by shooting you, at your discretion. Which mode of death do you elect shall be inflicted upon you?"

Hopt—" I choose to be shot."

Shortly afterwards, going down the same street, I came upon another great crowd round a photographer's, and I was told that imme-

MAIN STREET.

diately after Hopt had received his sentence he had been conveyed here to have his portrait taken. Whether this was at his "own discretion," or by order of the authorities, I could not ascertain.

Salt Lake City has a population of 30,000 inhabitants, of whom 25,000 are "Latter-day Saints," and 5,000 Gentiles, and just now the Gentiles seem to be making the city too hot for the saints. I was told that several of the leading men, including President Taylor, were wanted by the city marshals on the score of polygamy, but could not be found; and that one hundred polygamists are now in "The Pen," undergoing six months' imprisonment (and a fine of 300 dollars and costs) for refusing to part with their surplus wives.

Of the three men sentenced this day, the first was a policeman named Smith, who stood to his colours, as will be seen.

"THE COURT—Your name is Andrew Smith, I believe.

"MR. SMITH—Yes, sir.

"THE COURT—You have been found guilty of the crime of unlawful cohabitation, and this morning was fixed upon for your sentence. Have you anything to say why this sentence of the law should not be pronounced in accordance with the verdict—have you anything further to say?

"Mr. Smith then said, in a firm, clear voice—If your honour please: I have been placed on trial here for living in the practice of my religion, which I do not intend to relinquish, under any circumstances whatever, and I have no promises to make. Therefore, I am prepared to receive the judgment of the court. I cannot under any circumstances give up any principle of my religion. My religion is worth everything to me, or it is worth nothing, and I am prepared to receive any judgment you may see fit to pronounce. That is about all, I believe.

"The Court—I understand you to state by inference that you understand your religion authorizes you and makes it your duty to practice polygamy and unlawful cohabitation?

"Mr. Smith—That is a part and portion of my religion.

"The Court—Yes, and I suppose from what you state also that it makes it your duty to advise others, so far as you give any advice at all, to practise that?

"Mr. Smith—I have not been an adviser, sir, but that is my feeling. I am not much of a preacher; but my religion is worth everything to me. As I said before, I could not sacrifice that under any consideration whatever.

"The Court—Well, I have so often stated here from this bench that polygamy and unlawful cohabitation are crimes under the laws of the United States that it is hardly worth while to state it again. I presume you understand that they are both defined as crimes, and you must realize that you are not to determine what the laws of the United States are for yourself, contrary to the tribunals selected to interpret and construe the laws and to enforce them. In view of your statements the law makes it my duty to impose upon you such a penalty as may possibly reform you and may tend to deter others from like crimes against society. The object of this law is to protect society, and it is my duty to enforce that law so far as the law gives me my discretion, and use the discretion which I possess so as to accomplish the purpose and to reach the end intended by the law. You are sentenced in the penalty of a term of six months, and to pay a fine of 300 dollars and costs. You will also stand committed until the fine and costs are paid."

The next defendant was evidently a gentleman of considerable standing in the city.

"As the name of John Nicholson was called, there was a buzz of interest which subsided into a breathless silence as that gentleman stood up under the judge's gaze.

"THE COURT—Mr. Nicholson, I suppose it is hardly necessary for me to state to you—you are already advised that the jury found you guilty of the crime of unlawful cohabitation. Have you anything further to say why sentence of the law should not be pronounced against you?

"MR. NICHOLSON—If your honour please: I will take advantage of the privilege that the court affords me of stating my position before the court from my own standpoint. I have been connected with the Church of Jesus Christ of Latter-day Saints for about a quarter of a century. I accepted its doctrines, including the law that is called in the church 'celestial marriage,' which includes plurality of wives. At the time that I entered upon that relationship I had not the slightest idea that I was infringing upon or acting in contravention to any law made in pursuance of the constitution of the country, the supreme law of the land. I entered into that relation in 1871, and, to give the court an idea of my position in reference to the law, I will illustrate it by stating that when the Reynolds case was offered in order to test the constitutionality of the statute of 1862, enacted against polygamy, at the request of the defendant in that suit I went upon the stand and testified for the prosecution that a conviction might be obtained. There is no need for me to state to your honour that the essence of a crime is the intent to commit it. There could be no intention on my part to commit a crime in entering into the relationship which I have mentioned.

"Years afterwards the Edmunds' law was enacted, which made my status criminal—that is to say, from my standpoint—my conduct was made by it *malum prohibitum*, because in my opinion it cannot be made *malum in se*. That law requires that I should give up a vital principle of my religion, and discard at least a portion of my family, and consequently disrupt my family organization.

"This places me, as your honour will perceive, in a

very painful position : because I have a large family, and the ties which bind them to myself are sacred, and the affection which I entertain for them is deep, and I do not think that these ties can possibly be severed by any law of whatever character it may be, or from whatever source it may spring ; because there are sentiments and feelings that are engendered in the human heart that the law cannot touch. I will say here, also, that the lady who would have been the principal witness in this case, had I not testified against myself, stated to me that she would decline to testify against me, or do anything that would have the effect of sending me to prison. And now, after such an exhibition of devotion to me on her part, the bare contemplation of cutting her adrift is revolting to my soul, and I could not do it.

" People's ideas differ in regard to what constitutes religion. Some hold that it is merely sentiment and faith, and does not necessarily embody action. I differ from this view ; and I have always been bold to express my opinions on every subject without fear, favour, or hope of reward. I am of the opinion expressed by the Apostle James, who stated that faith without works is dead. The religion that I believe in is a religion that finds expression in action.

" I am aware of the attitude of the court, and I presume of the country, towards the peculiar institution of religion in the Church with which I am identified, and which I have honestly accepted and have honestly practised. It is held that this conjugal relationship threatens the existence of monogamous marriage.

must say that, judging from the attitude of this court, which represents, I presume, the attitude of the nation, and in view of the assaults that are made on plural marriage, it appears to me that there is not very much ground for apprehension of danger in that respect.

"It is also true that some people hold that my relations in a family capacity are adulterous. From my point of view, however, I have the consoling reflection that I am in excellent company, including Moses, the enunciator, under God, of the principles which constitute the foundation of modern jurisprudence.

"Not to weary the court, I will simply say that my purpose is fixed, and I hope unalterable. It is, that I shall stand by my allegiance to God, fidelity to my family, and what I conceive to be my duty to the constitution of the country, which guarantees the fullest religious liberty to the citizen.

"I thank your honour for bearing with me, and will now simply conclude by stating that I am prepared to receive the pleasure of the court.

"Mr. Nicholson spoke in a low, but clear and deliberate tone, which was maintained without variation to the close. The manner, as much as the matter of his speech, clearly prepossessed all hearers in his favour, and even the judge was impressed by it."

It will be seen from these examples that there is a strong determination on the part of the United States' government to root out polygamy, and there also seems to be an equally firm determination of the Mormons to stand by this, which they regard as an essential article of faith.

After a long address from the judge, Mr. Nicholson and the other polygamists received the same sentence as Smith, and were all driven off to the Penitentiary.

It may be added that a Bill now before Congress is of a still more stringent character. I quote the following from a recent evening paper:—

" The Bill provides that all marriages in the Territories shall be certified in writing by the minister and contracting parties, compels the testimony of the husband or wife of the accused in prosecutions for polygamy, prescribes punishment for adultery in Utah, and abolishes the present limitation of prosecutions for adultery to the complaint of husband or wife. It also abolishes female suffrage, takes away the general jurisdiction of the Utah probate courts, and annuls the territorial law about the capacity of illegitimate children to inherit property. The Bill further attacks the Mormon Church by giving the President of the United States authority to appoint trustees to take charge of its temporal affairs, and annuls the Mormon emigration fund, prohibiting the re-establishment of any such corporation for importing Mormons, all funds being forfeited for the benefit of a school fund in Utah."

We paid a visit to the Tabernacle, the Temple, and Assembly Hall. We were politely received by the superintendent, who showed us round in the usual way. The wonderful acoustic properties of the Tabernacle, by which a pin dropped at one end of the great building can be distinctly heard at the other, were pointed out. I quote the following brief statistics about these buildings, only remarking that, judged by present appearances, the Temple is not likely to be completed for many years :—

Tabernacle : This building is 233 feet long, 133 feet wide, and 70 feet high. It has 20 doors of 9 feet wide. In case of an accident an audience of 10,000 people can be cleared out in a few minutes. Seating capacity, 12,000.

Temple : The corner-stone was laid April 12th, 1853, and amount expended in construction to March 12th, 1884, $2,500,000. It is 200 by 800 feet. Height of walls, 100 feet. Middle tower on either end will be 200 feet high.

Assembly Hall : Dimensions of building, 120 by 68 feet. Seating capacity, 2,500. Cost, $150,000. Services every Sunday at 2 p.m. The ceiling is divided off into sixteen panels of different shape and design, each panel having some fresco painting ; one of them is a rather gaudy-looking historical painting of "The angel Moroni showing the prophet Joseph where the plates were hid in the hill Cumorah."

Bee-Hive, Lion, and Gardo Houses: One block east of the Temple, the latter block now occupied by President John Taylor.

Streets: There are nearly 100 miles of streets in Salt Lake City. They run with the four points of the compass. Each street is 132 feet wide, including the side-walks, and nearly all are bordered with shade trees. A small stream of water also flows down each side of many streets.

Total population of Utah in 1880, 143,965. Population of Salt Lake City is about 30,000.

Value of Utah's mineral production in 1884 is estimated at $9,301,508.

Great Salt Lake is nearly 100 miles long by 60 miles wide, with average depth of 40 feet.

In the afternoon we drove round the city and suburbs, and up to Fort Douglas, a well-built full-regiment post, situated on a plateau three miles east of the city. It is well laid out, and the officers' quarters, in charming little villas embowered in creepers and green foliage, are exceedingly pleasant to look at.

Our driver was an Englishman, a thirty-years' resident, who had married a Mormon wife (now dead), but he was careful to tell us that he was and always had been a Gentile, though for the sake of peace and quietness, and, in the early days, personal safety, he had duly paid his " tithing." He prided himself in having driven Hepworth Dixon during his stay here, and in having " introduced " Lord Carrington to President Taylor! The stories he volunteered to tell us were perhaps more facetious than veracious.

I will only add that the city in its outward appearance has left a most favourable impression on me—it is pleasantly situated at the foot of the Wasatch Mountains, which rise on the east to a height of from 10,000 to 12,000 feet, and are covered with snow nearly all the year. The city occupies a series of terraces, and, with its houses half hidden in shade and fruit-trees, it presents the appearance of a beautiful green oasis in the midst of a desert.

CLIFFS OF ECHO CAÑON.

LETTER No. XV.

Leave for Cheyenne—"Rock Springs"—Murder of Chinese—Mr. Black's "Green Pastures" and bottle of champagne—"Hell upon Wheels"--Big Horn Cowboy and Milord.

Cheyenne, Oct., 1885.

WE left Salt Lake City by the Union Pacific Railway on Wednesday at 7.50 a m., and we reached Cheyenne at 10.30 a.m. on Thursday. It is impossible for me to describe or even to mention the many objects of interest and points of beautiful scenery through which this line passes. How can one describe in a few hurried words such scenes as those to be found in "The Echo Cañon," "The Devil's Gate," "The Devil's

Gate Mountain," and "The Devil's Slide"?[1] The makers of this road, or the early pioneers,

"THE DEVIL'S SLIDE," WEBER CAÑON.

[1] It will be remembered that the Devil has another slide in the Yellowstone Park.

seem to have had a great liking for his black majesty, or they would not have given his name to such splendid scenery.

About two hundred miles east of Ogden we passed a place called "Rock Springs," where a number of Chinamen had been brutally massacred by white miners a week or two before.

Two Chinamen had taken up a white man's "chamber," and when ordered out the Chinamen went at them with their picks. A general battle ensued, in which two men were shot. At night their village was set fire to, and it was said that several Chinamen in trying to escape from the fire were shot down by the miners, and about fifteen others perished in the flames.

Soldiers from the nearest fort were sent for, and several miners were arrested, but it was found impossible to get sufficient evidence to convict them. The Chinese Consul from Washington had just been there investigating the brutal affair, and was returning in the same train with us.

In Mr. William Black's "Green Pastures and Piccadilly" there is an interesting description of Cheyenne as it was some twelve years ago. There was a time, not long previous to Mr. Black's visit, when this now thriving little city had earned for itself the name of "Hell upon Wheels," and I was told by an inhabitant who lived there then, when the Union Pacific Railway was being made, and the city comprised a long row of saloon tents, that bowie knives and six-shooters were freely used in the settlement of disputes, and that three or four murders a week were the average, to say nothing of fights with Sioux Indians.

Cheyenne had settled down from these exciting times when Mr. Black arrived there, and he found "nothing about its outward appearance to entitle anyone to call it 'Hell on Wheels.'"

"Certainly," he says, "the Cheyenne we saw was far from being an exciting place; there was not a single corpse lying at any of the saloon doors, nor any duel being fought in the street."

Of the outskirts of Cheyenne, he says :—

"The odd fashion in which shanties and sheds with some private houses here and there—are dotted down anyhow on the plain; their temporary look; the big advertisements; the desolate and homeless appearance of the whole place, all serve to recall the dismal scene that is spread around the Grand Stand on Epsom Downs on the morning after Derby Day, when the revellers have all returned to town. . . . We drove out to a lake which will no doubt form an ornamental feature in a big park, when the Black Hill miners, gorged with wealth, come back to make Cheyenne a great city."

Mr. Black will be pleased to know that his prophecy has been, to some extent, fulfilled.

Cheyenne is now a most pleasant city. The big park has been formed; the streets are broad, and lined with trees; the houses are well-built; there are stores there which would almost rival Whiteley's or Shoolbred's in the magnitude and variety of their contents, and perhaps surpass them in their outward appearance. The outskirts are now dotted, I might rather say crowded, with very charming "Queen Anne" villas, surrounded by well-laid-out lawns, flower-beds, and creeping foliage, reminding one not so much of Epsom Downs, as of that æsthetic suburb of London known as Bedford Park, only that the houses are larger and better built, and in their furniture display an exuberance of wealth and good taste. There are two fine hotels, several churches and chapels, and a delightful little club-house, where we were most hospitably entertained.

I may add that the place has none of the appearance of vulgar show which "Black Hill miners, gorged with wealth," might be supposed to have given to it; on the contrary, it has an air of quiet respectability not to be seen in many other western cities. The inhabitants are well-educated people, musical and social, and amongst them is a large community of well-bred English people.

As I have a personal interest in the matter, I will venture to give another extract from "Green Pastures and Piccadilly."

Mr. Black says that—

"As he was unanimously requested by his party to pay a tribute of gratitude to the clean and comfortable inn at the station, he must now do so; only he must also confess that he was bribed, for the good-natured landlord was pleased, as we sat at supper, to send in to us, with his compliments, a bottle of real French champagne. Good actions should never go unrewarded; so the gentle reader is most earnestly entreated, the first time he goes to Cheyenne, to stay at this inn and give large orders. Moreover, the present writer not wishing to have his conduct in this particular regarded as being too mercenary, would wish to explain that the bottle of champagne in question was, as was subsequently discovered, charged for in the bill and honestly paid for too ; but he cannot allow the landlord to be deprived of all credit for his hospitable intentions merely on account of an error on the part of the clerk."

Just before I left England, and knowing that I contemplated a visit to the Rockies, Mr. Black was good enough to request me to look into his book and to see, from the circumstances, as quoted above, whether I was not fairly entitled to have that bottle of champagne produced : he also desired me to present his compliments to a "very pretty Scotch lassie" at the hotel.

Of course I pursued the inquiry; I had by chance stayed at this very hotel, but I ascertained, alas! that poor old Jones, the good-natured landlord, had long since made his pile in the good old times when he could charge crowds of passengers a dollar and a half for their meals instead of (as now) seventy-five cents only; had retired to a farm somewhere in Idaho; had died, and left an enormous fortune to his widow. I may also inform Mr. Black that "the pretty Scotch lassie" is now the mother of a large family somewhere up in the mountains.

The inn has become the property of the Union Pacific, and is, in fact, one of the dining stations of that enterprising company. I regret to say that the intelligent and civil manager, though perfectly acquainted with the circumstances (through having read "Green Pastures" in a ten cent edition), did not feel it to be a part of his duty to his employers to hand over to me the bottle of champagne, notwithstanding the credentials I presented. He did not, however, raise the slightest objection when I invited him to join me and my friend M. in drinking to the health of the writer of "Green Pastures," to the wealthy widow of the departed Jones, and to "the pretty Scotch lassie," wherever she may be.

A local newspaper thus, somewhat erroneously, recorded our visit to this city:—

"A. B. and C. D., two Englishmen who have been travelling around the world, stopped off yesterday morning, and are guests at The Pacific. They had letters of introduction to Jones(!), the former landlord of the hotel, and had been told that Cheyenne was 'Hell on Wheels.' They are disappointed."

In these western parts it is a dangerous thing sometimes to refuse a "drink," and to offer to pay for it is a mortal offence. I was told that in Cheyenne even the cowboys, with their big whips, broad-brimmed felt hats, and hip-joint boots, were a superior, well-educated class, who had a large reading-room, crowded of an evening with men who could hold their own on any subject, political, social, or literary; and that there were among them good mathematicians, and even classical scholars.

The following cutting from "The Cheyenne Democrat" exhibits the cowboy in another light:—

"HE DRANK.

"MILORD HAS AN ADVENTURE WITH A BIG HORN COWBOY AND A BIG HORN.

" Editor Becker, of the Big Horn 'Sentinel,' tells a good story of a nobby and snobby milord, of British extraction, who travelled from Big Horn with him and Abe Idelman on the stage-coach early this week.

Milord was excessively exclusive. He wouldn't be social, and spoke to no one except the two 'John Henry' servants he had with him, and was altogether as unpleasant as his snobbishness could make him. At a dinner station there were a lot of jolly cowboys on a lark, and one of them 'treating' everybody asked the Englishman to drink. Of course, milord haughtily refused. The cowboy displayed a dangerous-looking six-shooter, and very impressively insisted on his drinking.

"'But I cawn't, you know. I don't drink, you know,' was milord's reply.

"Mr. Cowboy brought the muzzle in dangerous proximity to the knot in which milord's brains were supposed to lie hidden somewhere, and then he said he'd drink—he'd take soda water, you know.

"'Soda water nuthin,' said Mr. Cowboy. 'You'll take straight whiskey.'

"'But, aw, this American whiskey, I cawn't swallow it, you know.'

"'Well,' said the cowboy, 'I'll make a hole in the side of your head so that we can pour it in,' and he began to draw down on milord, and milord said—

"'Aw, that'll do; I'll drink it.'

"Then the cowboy invited milord's servants to drink, which horrified him.

"'They don't drink, you know,' he said.

"'Well, we'll see whether they do or not,' said Mr. Cowboy. 'The chances are you don't give 'em a "hopportunity." Come up here, you fellows, and guzzle some,' and the two 'John Henrys,' with a little show of reluctance, but really glad to get a drink, came up, and the cowboy passed a tumbler full of torchlight procession whiskey for milord, and the servants poured for themselves. Then the cowboy made the 'John Henrys' clink glasses with milord, and all drank, and there was great fun. Milord tried after that to be very jolly, and the stimulant assisted him decidedly. But in the coach he fell back into his exclusiveness and retained it throughout, and has probably got it yet.

"Now the fact is that, abstractly, the cowboy was wrong in forcing a man to drink who had no desire to do so. But, on the other hand, snobbishness is not the proper thing in this country, and sensible men generally try, while in Rome, to do as Rome does. At any rate, they don't make themselves offensive to the country in which they are travelling."

LETTER No. XVI.

We leave Cheyenne—Arrival at Omaha—The barber's shop—Narrow escape from having my head shaved—Arrival at Chicago—Niagara Falls.

New York, Nov., 1885.

I HAVE already told you that I am not writing a book of travels, but merely recording my impressions by the way; these have already occupied far more space than I had ever contemplated, and as we are now approaching the more beaten tracks of civilization, I will hasten on to a conclusion.

We left Cheyenne on Friday morning at 10.30, and after a continuous run of 516 miles, we "stopped off" at Omaha for a few hours at 10.30 on Saturday morning. Omaha is a great rambling city of 60,000 inhabitants on the western bank of the Missouri. Council Bluffs is an equally flourishing city on the eastern bank.

My chief recollection of Omaha is the barber's shop whither I went to get shaved. I had tried to shave myself in the train, but had contrived instead to gash my cheek sufficiently to cause much bloodshed. When the barber had finished shaving me, I asked him just to trim my hair the least bit in the world. He was an hour and a quarter over the job, and as I had been travelling continuously for twenty-four hours with little or no sleep, I fell asleep under his hands. Luckily, I was woke up by an unusual tickling at the back of my head ; he was lathering me there, and I am quite sure he meant to shave the whole of my head.

"Confound it," I shouted ; " what are you doing?"

" I was only going to shave the back of your head," he said.

I found to my horror that my whiskers had entirely disappeared, and he had not only cut my hair as closely as it could be cut with a pair of scissors, but he had run it over with a sort of small horse-clipper. I caught him in time to stop the further operation of shaving. Judging by the many naked polls I afterwards saw in the hotel, I concluded that it is the fashion in Omaha to go about with your head shaved. It is a compliment, I suppose, which those who have hair pay to the bald-headed ones.

The Omaha barber has quite destroyed the youthful appearance which I flattered myself I had acquired since I have been travelling on this Continent.

My friend M., when I came out of that terrible barber's hands, passed me by without knowing me; and when at last he began to have a suspicion that the bald individual before him was I, he exclaimed, "What on earth have you been doing? An hour and a quarter of our precious time have you wasted in that barber's shop, and you come out like a bald-headed boiled lobster. Our friends in Chicago, Boston, and New York certainly won't know you."

Time the destroyer is also a happy restorer, and now while I am writing, a fortnight after the event, my whiskers have already given indication of a returning crop, and my hair has grown long enough to enable me to identify myself. I trust that after the sea voyage, and when I get home, my wife will also be able to identify me. The rascal charged me seventy-five cents (three shillings) for this personal disfigurement.

I was very glad to get away from Omaha the same day at 5.30 p.m. We travelled by the Chicago and Rock Island line, and we reached Chicago, a distance of 500 miles, the next afternoon at three o'clock.

On Monday it rained in torrents all day, and Tuesday was not much better. On Tuesday night at 8.40 I started for Boston, leaving my friend M. behind for two or three days. This was the first time we had separated since we started together from Euston on our outward journey.

The line I now travelled on was "The Michigan Central." About seven o'clock next morning we reached Niagara, where the train stopped a few minutes to give us a look at "The Falls."

As I have no more superlative adjectives left in my vocabulary, I will tell you what the "Michigan Central" has to say about Niagara. It far surpasses my most sublime efforts.

"THE NIAGARA FALLS ROUTE.

"'So long as the waters of that mighty river thunder down to the awful depths below, so long as the rush and roar, the surge and foam, and prismatic spray of nature's cataractic masterpiece remain to delight and awe the human soul, thousands and tens of thousands of beauty-lovers and grandeur-worshippers will journey over the only railroad from which it can be seen. *There is but one Niagara Falls on earth, and but one direct great railway to it.*'

"Trains stop at Falls View, near the brink of the Horseshoe Fall, where the finest view is obtainable without leaving the cars, cross the gorge of Niagara river on the great steel, double-track Cantilever Bridge, the greatest triumph of modern engineering, and connect in Union Depots, at Niagara Falls and Buffalo with the New York Central and Hudson River, the only four-track railroad in the world."

CONCLUSION.

Home, Dec. 9, 1885.

HERE is no place like home, after all. On reaching Boston, I felt more like being at home than I had ever felt since I left my own country. Boston resembles an old English city more than any other town I have yet visited in America.

It is, however, no part of my plan to describe the "Hub." I think it is Benjamin Disraeli who says somewhere that "description is always a bore both to the describer and the describee," and I have sinned enough in this direction already; nor have I any desire to make intrusive and impertinent remarks about the inhabitants. I will only say that the few days I spent in Boston were made very pleasant by the most courteous and unostentatious hospitality.

From the classic city I passed on to the Empire City, as New York is sometimes called. I was told long before I left England by warmhearted friends in New York that if I ever visited that city their utmost should be done " to impair my digestion !" They did their best, and I hereby declare my gratitude to them for their generous intentions. Suffice it to say that I eventually got away from them with no more serious injury than could be cured by a few days' tossing and rolling on the broad Atlantic.

Our passage was even rougher and more trying on the whole than the outward passage had been, but we did not mind that; for were we not homeward bound?

I have now been at home about three weeks, and I am already beginning to doubt whether it is an actual fact that such a stay-at-home old fixture as I have always been, could, within the last four months, have travelled something like fourteen thousand miles by land and sea! I am inclined to regard that great land of my pilgrimage as altogether

> "The land of vision; it would seem
> A still, an everlasting dream!"

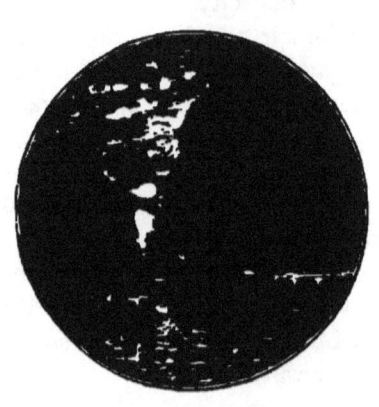

APPENDIX.

HE following information is supplied by the Northern Pacific Railroad Company.

How to obtain Government Land.

There are over 40,000,000 acres of the best Government lands in America located in the extremely fertile regions of Minnesota, North Dakota, Montana, Northern Idaho, Washington, and Oregon, and traversed by the Northern Pacific Railroad, open for occupancy by actual settlers. The laws of the United States provide that citizens of the United States, or persons who have declared their intention to become such, can obtain lands as follows:

PRE-EMPTIONS.

Heads of families, widows or single persons (male or female) over the age of twenty-one years, who are citizens of the United States, or who have declared their intention to become such under the naturalization laws, may enter upon any "offered" or "unoffered" lands belonging to the United States, or any unsurveyed lands to which the Indian title has been extinguished, outside of the limits of any land grant, and purchase not exceeding 160 acres under the pre-emption laws. If the tract is "offered" land, the settler must file his "declaratory statement" in the United States District Land Office within thirty days after making settlement; and within one year from the date of settlement he must make proof of actual residence on and cultivation of the land, and thereupon purchase the same at $1.25 per acre, if outside of the limits of a railroad land grant, and at $2.50 per acre if within railroad land grant limits. If the tract is "unoffered" land, the settler must file his "declaratory statement" within three months from the date of settlement, and make final proof and payment within thirty-three months from the date of settlement. If the tract is unsurveyed land, the declaratory statement must be filed within three months after the approved plat of the township is received at the United States District Land Office, and final proof and payment must be made within thirty months after the expiration of the said three months. A pre-emptor may submit proofs of continuous residence at any time after six months from the date of settlement, and obtain title to his land. The settler in possession of a valid pre-emption claim may, at any time, convert his pre-emption claim into a homestead. No person who abandons his residence upon land of his own (not a town lot) to reside upon public lands in the same state or territory, or who owns 320 acres of land in any state or territory, is entitled to the benefits of the pre-emption laws.

HOMESTEADS.

Any person who is the head of a family, or who has arrived at the age of twenty-one years, and is a citizen of the United States, or has filed his declaration of intention to become such, is entitled to enter one-quarter section, or less quantity of unappropriated public land, under the homestead laws. The applicant must make affidavit that he is entitled to the privileges of the homestead act, and that the entry is made for his exclusive use and benefit, and for actual settlement and cultivation, and must pay the legal fee and that part of the commissions required as follows: Fee for 160 acres, $10; commission, $4 to $12; fee for eighty acres, $5; commission, $2 to $6. Within six months from the date of entry, the settler must take up his residence upon the land, and reside thereupon and cultivate the same for five years continuously. At the expiration of this period, or within two years thereafter, proof of residence and cultivation must be established by four witnesses. The proof of settlement with the certificate of the Registrar of the Land Office is forwarded to the General Land Office at Washington, from which patent is issued. Final proof cannot be made until the expiration of five years from date of entry, and must be made within seven years. The Government recognizes no sale of a homestead claim. A homestead settler may at any time purchase the land under the pre-emption laws if desired, upon making proof of settlement and cultivation for a period of not less than six months from the date of entry to the time of purchase. The law allows only one homestead privilege to any one person.

Timber Culture Claims.

Under the timber culture laws, public lands naturally devoid of timber may be acquired by planting trees thereon, and keeping the same in a healthy, growing condition for eight years. Not more than 160 acres in any one section can be entered, and no person can enter more than 160 acres or make more than one entry under these laws. An applicant must be the head of a family or twenty-one years of age, and a citizen of the United States, or he must have filed his declaration of intention to become a citizen, as required by the naturalization laws. The Land Office fee for an entry of more than 80 acres is $14; and for 80 acres or less, $9; and $4

P

when final proof is made. Land to be entered must be entirely devoid of timber. In order to acquire 160 acres of land, 10 acres must be cultivated and planted with trees ; 5 acres must be cultivated and planted with trees to acquire any legal subdivision of 80 acres ; and 2½ acres to acquire any legal subdivision of 40 acres or less. The person making entry of 160 acres is required to break or plough five acres during the first year, and five acres during the second year. The five acres broken or ploughed during the first year must be cultivated to crop or otherwise during the second year, and be planted to timber during the third year. The five acres broken or ploughed the second year must be cultivated the third year, and planted to timber the fourth year. For entries of less than 160 acres, a proportionate number of acres must be ploughed, planted, cultivated and planted to trees. These trees must be cultivated and protected for not less than eight years ; and at the expiration of that period, or within five years thereafter, proof must be made by the claimant and two credible witnesses, showing that there were at the time of making such proof at least 675 living, thrifty trees on each of the ten acres required to be planted; also that not less than 2,700 trees were planted on each of the ten acres. Fruit-trees are not considered timber, within the meaning of this act. Title cannot be obtained prior to the expiration of eight years, and final proof must be made within five years after the expiration of the said eight years.

Desert Land.

Any person who is a citizen of the United States, or any person of requisite age who may be entitled to become a citizen, and who has filed his declaration to become such, may file his oath with the Registrar and Receiver of the Land Office in the district in which any desert land is located, that he intends to reclaim, not exceeding one section of said land, by conducting water upon it, within three years; and by paying to the Receiver twenty-five cents. per acre for all the land claimed, such person may enter said land under the desert land act. At any time within three years a patent can be obtained by making proof that he has reclaimed said land, and paying the additional sum of $1 per acre. No person can enter more than one tract of land, and not to exceed 640 acres, which shall be in a compact form. This act applies to desert lands in Dakota, Montana, Idaho, Washington, and Oregon.

Desert lands are defined by this act to be all lands, exclusive of mineral and timber lands, which will not without irrigation produce some agricultural crop.

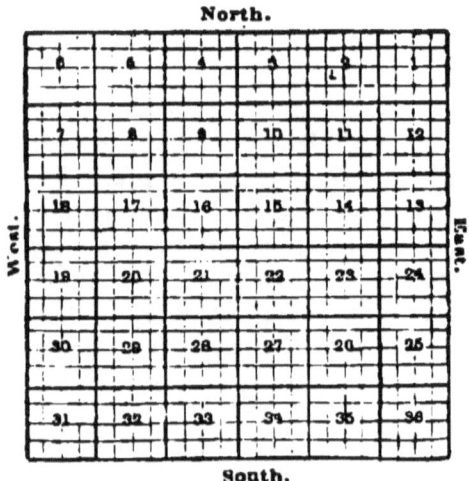

The above is a diagram of a township, with sections numbered according to government surveys.

APPENDIX. 213

A township is 6 miles square and contains 36 square miles, or 36 sections, each section being 1 mile square, and containing 640 acres of land.

A quarter section is one-half mile square, 160 acres. An acre of land is 208.71 feet square, and contains 43,560 square feet. Sections 16 and 36 in Dakota, Montana, and Washington are reserved for school purposes.

GOVERNMENT LAND OFFICES

In Districts tributary to the Northern Pacific Railroad and Allied Lines.

Minnesota.	Dakota.	Montana.
St. Cloud.	Fargo.	Miles City.
Fergus Falls.	Grand Forks.	Bozeman.
Crookston.	Bismarck.	Helena.
Duluth.		
Taylor's Falls.	Lewiston, Idaho Ty.	

Washington.	Oregon.
Olympia.	Oregon City.
Vancouver.	Roseburg.
Walla Walla.	La Grande.
Spokane Falls.	Lake View.
North Yakima.	The Dalles.

214   *APPENDIX.*

The following diagram shows the difference of time on the American continent :—

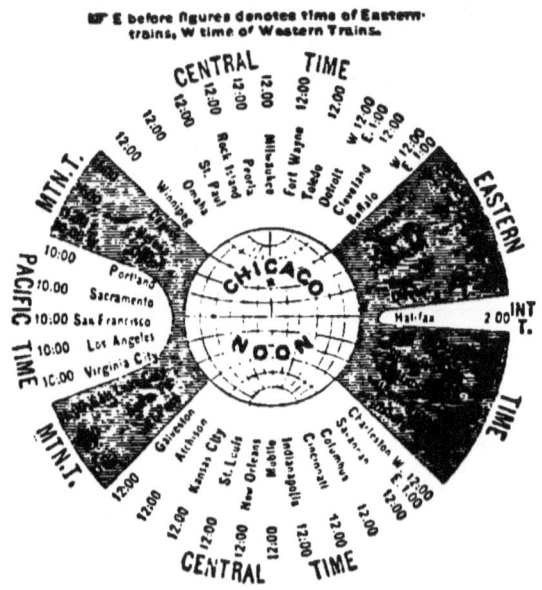

INFORMATION FOR SETTLERS

IN THE

NORTHERN PACIFIC COUNTRY.

Giving Suggestions relating to Farming Implements, Fuel, Animals, Household Goods, Lumber, Breaking New Prairie, Location of Markets, and other valuable Information.

The best time to come to the NORTHERN PACIFIC COUNTRY is in the spring, but farmers can come to this favoured region at any season, properly outfitted, and in a short time acquire a comfortable and prosperous home.

The breaking season extends from about May 15th to July 15th. Three horses or mules, or two yoke of oxen, constitutes a good breaking team for a sulky or walking plough.

Sowing grain commences as soon as the frost is out of the ground to the depth of a few inches. The work is generally begun about April 1st, and completed in 10 to 15 days. Some years the grain can be put in as early as March 20th.

Good farm horses can be bought at from $100 to $150, according to size, &c. Cows are worth from $25 to $40 each, and working oxen from $90 to $125 per yoke. Standard makes of farm wagons cost $60. Breaking costs, usually, from $2.50 to $3.00 per acre, and back-setting $1.50 to $1.75. The settler opening a new farm can always find plenty of work among his neighbours, after he has done his own breaking and back-setting, and cut his hay. He can raise an abundance of vegetables from the sod the first year. From 150 to 200 bushels potatoes, and from 25 to 45 bushels of oats can be raised on the sod the first year. Good common lumber ranges from $20 to $25 per thousand along the line of the railroad. Car load lots, for settlers, are carried by the railroad at the same rates given to dealers. A good house can be built for $350 to $700. Household goods, farm implements and working stock can be bought at reasonable prices at St. Paul and Minneapolis, and at various points along the road.

Liberal provision is made by law for schools, and, in the towns and country settlements, school-houses and churches of the several denominations abound. The people who come to this country believe in these institutions.

There is an abundance of cheap fuel supplied from the great

coalfields of North Dakota and Montana, and also from the extensive forests of Northern Minnesota, Western Montana, Northern Idaho, Washington, and Oregon. Good water abounds all along the line of the Northern Pacific Railroad.

There is a combination of soil and climate in the Northern Pacific country which makes it the most reliable and productive wheat region in the world, and in no other section of the United States have there been, for so many consecutive years, such bountiful crops. It is as healthy a country as there is in America. There is always a market for farm products at good prices. Quick and cheap transportation is afforded by the lake port at Duluth, or by rail direct, to the great markets of the world ; while the numerous mining camps in the RICH GOLD AND SILVER SECTION through which the Northern Pacific Railroad passes, afford a western market at good prices. The United States Government is also a large purchaser of oats, hay and provisions in North Dakota and Montana for use at the various military posts. The immense flouring mills at Minneapolis and other points, which grind over 24,000,000 bushels of wheat a year, are active bidders for the "**No. 1 Hard**" spring wheat grown along the Northern Pacific. The great wheat belt which produces the celebrated hard spring wheat Scotch Fife - which is acknowledged to be superior to any other variety grown, is traversed by the Northern Pacific Railroad for a distance of over 600 miles, through Northern Minnesota and North Dakota.

Reduced rates of fare are given land seekers, and reduced rates of fare and freight to settlers in North Dakota.

Settlers will find people of their own nationality in the country along the Railroad, and the Land Department employs Norwegian, Swedish and German agents, who are ready to meet emigrants and give them all needed information and assistance.

There are splendid openings in this new and rapidly developing country for carpenters, painters, blacksmiths, plumbers, shoemakers, tailors, harness-makers, and workers at all other trades.

It costs more per acre for manure, lime and other fertilizers annually on many of the eastern farms than the best wheat lands in the Northern Pacific country cost per acre.

FREE! For Maps and Descriptive Publications, SENT FREE OF CHARGE, and for all information relating to lands and the Northern Pacific Country, apply to or address

P. B. GROAT,	or	CHAS. B. LAMBORN,
General Emigration Agent,		Land Commissioner,
ST. PAUL, MINN.		ST. PAUL, MINN.

THE BEST HOMES

For 10,000,000 People now await occupancy in Minnesota, North Dakota, Montana, Northern Idaho, Washington, and Oregon.

THE GREAT NEW NORTHERN PACIFIC COUNTRY.

2,000,000 Families **10,000,000 Souls!** Of the Great Population—no man can predict how great it will become—which will soon inhabit this vast region, the new comers from the older States wi'l become the first families, and leaders, socially and politically, in this newly opened section of the United States. They will all become prosperous, and many will acquire fortunes in a short period, by turning the vast wheat-producing lands, ready for the plough, into productive farms; by stock-raising, on the immense grazing ranges; by developing the resources of the extensive forests and mineral districts; by engaging in various trades and manufacturing enterprises; and by investments in the thriving new towns and other property in the vast region opened for settlement all along the line of the

NORTHERN PACIFIC RAILROAD.

LANDS! Millions and Millions of Acres of low-priced Lands for sale by the Northern Pacific Railroad Company on Easy Terms, and an equal amount of Government lands lying in alternate sections with the railroad land, are offered free to settlers, under the Homestead, Pre-emption and Tree Culture laws.

TERMS OF SALE OF NORTHERN PACIFIC RAILROAD LANDS.

Agricultural lands of the Company east of the Missouri River, in Minnesota and North Dakota, are sold chiefly at from $4.00 to $5.00 per acre, Grazing lands at from $3.00 to $4.00 per acre; and the preferred stock of the Company will be received at par in payment. When lands are purchased on **five years' time, one-sixth stock or cash** is required at time of purchase, and **the balance in five equal annual payments in stock or cash, with interest at 7 per cent.**

The price of agricultural lands in North Dakota west of the Missouri River, ranges chiefly from **$3 00 to 3 50 per acre**, and Grazing lands from **$2.00 to $2.50 per acre.** In Montana the price ranges chiefly from **$3 00 to $5 00 per acre** for Agricultural lands, and from **$1.25 to $2.50 per acre** for Grazing lands. If purchased on **five years' time** one-sixth cash, and the balance in five equal annual cash payments, with interest at 7 per cent. per annum.

The price of agricultural lands in Washington and Oregon ranges chiefly from **$2.60 to $6.00 per acre.** If purchased on **five years' time**, one-fifth cash. At end of first year the interest only on the unpaid amount. One-fifth of principal and interest due at end of next four years. Interest at 7 per cent. per annum.

On ten years' time.—Actual settlers can purchase not to exceed 320 acres of Agricultural land in **Minnesota, North Dakota, Montana, Idaho, Washington, and Oregon** on ten years' time at 7 per cent. interest, one-tenth cash at time of purchase and balance in nine equal annual payments, beginning at the end of the second year. At the end of the first year the interest only is required to be paid. Purchasers on the ten-year credit plan are required to settle on the land purchased and to cultivate and improve the same.

FREE! For Maps and Descriptive Publications, SENT FREE OF CHARGE, and for all information relating to lands and the Northern Pacific Country, apply to or address

P. B. GROAT, or **CHAS. B. LAMBORN,**
General Emigration Agent,   Land Commissioner,
ST. PAUL, MINN.   ST. PAUL, MINN.

AN AMATEUR ANGLER'S DAYS IN DOVE DALE.

BEING AN ACCOUNT OF MY THREE WEEKS HOLIDAY IN JULY AND AUGUST, 1884.

Imp. 32mo. fancy boards, 1s.; limp leather-cloth, gilt edges, 1s. 6d.

⁎⁎ *Also a Large Paper Edition, printed on hand-made paper parchment binding, price 5s. (all sold).*

OPINIONS OF THE PRESS.

The Athenæum says:—"This is an amusing little book, written with much brightness and considerable literary skill."

The Standard, *Dec.* 24, 1884:—"It is written in an exceptionally bright and genial style ... his writings bespeak an intense love of Nature and a keen power of observation. A strong vein of quiet humour runs through the volume, mingled with thoughts sometimes serious, sometimes playful. Altogether it is one of the most pleasantly written little books which we have read for a long time."

The Daily News says:—"Herein is the charm of the book. ... For an amateur, he certainly saturates you thoroughly with true Dove Dale flavour."

The Pall Mall Gazette:—"This is a pleasant book to read 'now that the fields are dank and ways are mire.'"

The World says:—"Not merely by brethren of the rod, but by all who appreciate Nature in her prettiest haunts it will be found pleasant reading."

The Illustrated News says:—"This charming bit of personal narrative ... will certainly be preserved on many a shelf where Izaak Walton and Charles Cotton hold the most honoured place."

The Graphic says:—"Written in a charming spirit, with plenty of quiet humour in it."

Harper's Magazine, *Jan.* 1885:—"He is *serus stud.orum*, he is only learning to fish, but he can write, and has made a very charming though brief addition to angling literature."

The Field says:—"Anyhow, the result of 'The Dove Dale Holidays' is a delightful pocket companion. . . . The principal charm of the little work is that it will be equally interesting to anglers and non-anglers."

The St. James's Gazette:—"Every page of it is good—a bright little volume. Worthy of gracious acceptance from all sorts and conditions of readers."

The Daily Telegraph:—"The fisherman, who must be as pleasant a companion by the waterside, as he is genial as an author, tells us how he spent three weeks' holidays, &c. . . . may employ very pleasantly half-an-hour of any angler's time."

The Guardian, *Nov.* 19, says:—"Tells in a very pleasant fashion how a delightful three weeks' holiday may be spent in beautiful Dove Dale."

Glasgow Herald:—"Decidedly interesting and amusing. It is gracefully and lightly written . . . he tells the story . . . with much quiet and quaint humour. . . . No angler should be without this excellent little book."

The Whitehall Review:—"This is one of the most charming little books we have met with for some time."

The St. Stephen's Review:—"No more charming little work than this has been published for many a day."

Army and Navy Gazette:—"A very pleasant little book."

Daily Chronicle:—"An entertaining little book."

Civil Service Gazette:—"This charming and interesting little book."

The Bookseller:—"A dainty little volume. . . . The author tells in a most charmingly simple style. . . . There is much quiet humour in the book. . . . The dedication is a little gem in its way."

The Literary World:—"Others besides anglers will read with interest this pleasant record of a holiday."

The Sunday Times says:—"One of those charming little *quasi-extempore* books. . . . We have enjoyed a very pleasant hour in reading."

The Publishers' Circular:—"All lovers of this picturesque scenery will welcome this fresh and natural tribute to its merits."

Lloyd's Weekly:—" A genial, pleasant little book, written in the happiest vein."

The Derby Mercury says:—" We have read no pleasanter book of its kind. . . . Always genial, sometimes humorous, sometimes thoughtful, sometimes playful, and invariably readable, displaying, though without parade, the signs of considerable culture."

Exeter and Plymouth Gazette:—"This is not the sort of bookmaker that the critic impales upon his hook. We hail him as the pleasant companion whose pleasant chat and merry companionship will beguile the hot hours," &c.

The Weekly Dispatch:—"A dainty little book by a disciple of Izaak Walton, who shows himself not unworthy to be named with his master, alike for steady handling of a line and for rambling use of a neat pen. He gossips pleasantly about the ins and outs of a corner of Derbyshire."

Land and Water:—"This is a very charming little book. . . . One of the brightest which we have read for many a long day, and we look forward to the publication of some more letters from the author."

Spectator:—" He seems to have got a good deal of pleasure out of his fishing; and something of this he is good enough to communicate to his readers."

The Banner:—"Tells most charmingly his successes as well as his failures."

Decoration:—"Out of very slight materials, by sheer charm of style, the author has succeeded in making a very fascinating book. . . . The author shows a cultured taste."

Warrington Guardian:—"An entertaining series of sketches."

Bath Herald:—" His descriptions of scenery and places of note are forcible without being laboured."

Western Daily Mercury:—" He is a more skilled handler of the pen than the rod, and his letters will be read with a great deal of pleasure, whether by anglers or by lovers of the picturesque in nature."

LONDON:
SAMPSON LOW, MARSTON, SEARLE, & RIVINGTON,
CROWN BUILDINGS, 188, FLEET STREET, E C.

ON READING "DAYS IN DOVEDALE BY AN AMATEUR ANGLER."

I.
Cheery, chatty, breezy booklet,
 Breathing scents of wilding flowers,
Cool and clear as mountain brooklet,
 Yet diffusing warmth of sunshine
  Thro' these wintry hours;

II.
Whence the power thy artless pages
 Have to soothe my weary brain,
Killing cares that Wisdom's sages,
 Flying philosophic maxims,
  Reason with in vain?

III.
Hence:—because, like him thou ownest
 With such modest grace, thy king,[1]
To the heart that's saddest, lonest,
 Needing healing, thou dost simply
  Nature's simples bring.

IV.
Nature's simples, God's specific,
 Pure and sweet as Cana's wine,
Flowing from His hand benefic,
 Fresh, by art left uncorrupted,
  Living blood of vine!—

V.
Making glad man's heart and lifting
 From it all its weight of care,
Till its sorrows seem like drifting
 Clouds that fly before the rising
  Of a mountain air.

VI.
Thanks for such a breeze, O writer,
 Blown from thy pure page to-night!
Night without its darkness, brighter
 Far than common days, for with thee
  I have walked in light;

VII.
Shared thy hope whilst thou hast angled,
 Nor could help a laugh, to see
All thy woes with line entangled,
 All thy flyless whippings, and thy
  Flight from angry bee!

VIII.
Felt a sympathetic sadness
 With thy disappointments: seen
With delight that sight of gladness—
 Age and infancy together
  Romping on the green!

IX.
O, with Lorna and with Alice,
 Far from stir and strife of men,
Rod in hand, refill thy chalice
 In the dales of Dove, and often
  Prythee write again!

COTSWOLD ISYS.

Jun 16th, 1885.   [1] Izaak Walton.

www.ingramcontent.com/pod-product-compliance
Lightning Source LLC
Chambersburg PA
CBHW031750230426
43669CB00007B/566